TALES OF T[illegible]R

A Collection o[illegible]tories

by

Fuad Matthew Caswell

By the same author under different names:

Matthew Caswell, Fuad Matthew Caswell, F. Matthew Caswell, and Dr. F. M. Caswell

Menashi's Boy.
The Slave Girls of Baghdad,
The Qiyān in the Early Abbasid Era.
Three Master Musicians.
Voices of the Arab Streets.
(in parts with Daphne Thomas) Stefan and Other Plays.
The Khamriyyāt of Abū Nuwās.

Mira Publishing House CIC.
Alfa House - Greenfield Court
Otley Rd. Leeds LS16 7TU – GB
www.MiraPublishing.com

Tales of the Near and Far
A collection of short stories
By: Fuad Matthew Caswell
ISBN: 978-1-908509-12-3
First published in Great Britain 2018 by Mira Publishing House CIC.

A full CIP record for this book is available from the British Library.
A full CIP record for this book is available from the Library of Congress.

For permission requests, please contact: info@mirapublishing.com
Find out more about the author and previous publications at www.fmcaswell.co.uk.
Produced in United Kingdom.

For the people of the Sinjar Mountains

Contents

About the Author

Fuad Matthew Caswell was born to a Baghdadi family and arrived in England as a student in 1950. He pursued courses of study at the University of London (SOAS and King's) followed by Oxford University (St. Catherine's Society). He acquired a BA in English and a London MA in Classical Arabic. He met and married a Yorkshire girl and they started a family, which coincided with several years spent setting up and running an import venture which was to continue as his Baghdadi family's business. The law always being his main interest, he then set out on the path of becoming a barrister, qualifying as a member of the Middle Temple in 1968. To improve his prospects of establishing a practice at the time, he adopted his wife's name Caswell and went on to have a long career as a barrister. In 2002 he returned to Oxford (Wadham), completing a doctorate in Arabic, the doctoral thesis appearing in print as *The Slave Girls of Baghdad: The Qiyan in the Early Abbasid Era.* .

Sandore

Suddenly, the thin mountain air was filled with the cry "Sabi", which cascaded down to the bottom of the valley and then rose to leave an echo on the other side. The villagers below stopped what they were doing to tell each other that Sabi was back. They craned their necks to see if they could discern anything high up on the path snaking down the mountain, they then turned to make their way to the mukhtar's house. The boys at play, among whom was the one who emitted the cry, stopped in their tracks and raced each other down the slope.

The young men who were harvesting the last of the apples and apricots lay down their baskets, left the orchards and followed the others. The women at the well gave the wet garments a last hurried pounding before gathering their baskets of washing, which they carried away on their heads. By the time a group of people had gathered outside the house of the mukhtar, the headman of Sandore, Jonah had already arrived and was sitting on a chair on the doorstep. As impassive and still as a stone statue, leaning on a walking stick wedged firmly in the ground, sightless eyes betraying no emotion, his mind fixed on a question: what had taken him so long?

The young mother held up a mirror to her face. She liked what she saw as she brushed and shook her tangled strands of golden hair. She bent down to open the wooden chest in the corner that held her trousseau. After carefully pulling out the garments that had been kept for a special occasion, she now started to put on her under-dress and puffy pants, full-length green gown adorned with beads, a gobarah belt made from metal coins in a chain, and a black velveteen hat decorated with turquoise beads. This was a special occasion, welcoming her husband, celebrating his safe return after an anxious wait, and presenting him with their newborn child. He was expected to be away for one week – that had now become almost a month.

Every year, the community's cash crop of apple and apricot would be gathered and taken to market in the nearest town to be replaced in return by the grain, rice and oil that would sustain the community throughout the winter.

For a long time, the task was carried out by one man who had acquired over the years the knowledge, business shrewdness and trading acumen that were required, and whose integrity was above reproach. Then he was killed in a tragic accident and a replacement had to be found.

There was more than one candidate and after an open discussion presided over by the mukhtar, they turned, as was often the case, to Jonah for a decision, which once made would be final. He pointed to Sabi. That surprised many since Sabi was a young man, not much older than a youth, untested in business, with hardly any experience of life beyond the valley and he had a young bride expecting their first child.

Soon, almost the whole community were in the road outside the mukhtar's house. They didn't take their eyes off the mountain and talked softly, almost in whispers. It was ever thus, an anxious moment in the yearly life in the valley. Every man, woman and child not knowing what would come down that path to them; the prices of apple, apricot, corn, rice and oil dependent on the vagaries of markets far beyond their valley and beyond their ken.

On this occasion the anxiety was so much greater. What with the youth and inexperience of Sabi, and the unexpected, as yet, unexplained delay.

There was a sudden stirring among them when they saw Sabi come into view from behind a bend. He looked so small as he walked in front of the lead mare followed by the other mules. Eyes were fixed on them, counting them for reassurance and surveying the bulging bags. As they got near, Sabi stopped. He rummaged in one of the bags, let loose the lead rope and, without looking right or left, walked straight ahead to where Jonah was sitting.

The latter, sensing the arrival of Sabi, held out his hand to receive a handful of corn. There was total stillness while the blind man felt the grains, smelt them and rubbed them between his palms. He picked one and lifted it to his mouth, crushed it between his teeth, then handed the grains back to Sabi before saying "*khosh*". With that word of approbation, the spell was broken.

The men milled around addressing Sabi with words of welcome and congratulations. The mukhtar directed some of the men to lead the mules to the back of the house and unload the bags in the communal storehouse where they would remain when the valley was covered in snow, the mountain paths unusable, and for the contents to be distributed as rations to every soul in the valley.

Sabi was detained by Jonah who wanted to know what had taken him so long. He explained that he went to Dhok first but was disappointed by what they offered. Later that night he met another man at the *khan* who was in the same predicament, so they decided to take their produce all the way to Arbil. He was interrupted in his narrative by his mother who came over and pulled him by the hand to where his wife was standing.

"Enough of that, you have a wife and son," she said cheerfully.

"A son?" he exclaimed.

"Yes, name him Yusuf, after your late father."

The young mother held up the child, which Sabi gathered in his arms.

"Yusuf," he exclaimed before starting down the hill towards their cottage. He pressed the child close to his chest, his wife following a pace behind. "Yusuf," he repeated to himself.

An old woman came out of her cottage to see what was happening. She saw them from a distance, gave a wide smile and pointed to the newborn baby. "M'barac Sabi," she called out congratulating the father.

The young mother called back, correcting her, "Abu Yusuf."

❋ ❋ ❋

Habiba

The first intimation that this was to be a special day was when she approached the well. There would usually be a gathering of girls drawing water as they gossiped. On this occasion they were standing still, pails on the ground, heads turned upwards. As she drew level with them, one engaged her attention.

"Look, look, Habiba," she said pointing, "it's the car coming back again."

Habiba could now see a car halfway up the hill resting where the meandering path petered out. It had been two years since a car was last seen in the valley. That was when cousin Lamis was taken away. There was now a flurry of girlish excitement, speculation, confused talk and debate.

"I wonder whose turn it is this time?"

"I wouldn't mind it being me."

"Why would I want it? Go away and not come back?"

"I would have nice clothes and an exciting life in the city."

"Wouldn't you miss your life here?"

"What's there to miss? There's nothing to keep us here."

The driver got out of the car wearing long, baggy trousers and a short, tight jacket over a striped shirt. A cummerbund wrapped round his waist suggested he was one of their people.

As he went to the first cottage, Habiba felt the palpitation of her heart. It was her home.

After a while, he came out and retraced his steps laboriously up towards the car. Her mother then came out. Her shrill call carried to Habiba who picked up her pail and dashed home where she quickly washed her hands and wiped her face clean as they waited to receive the visitors.

They were townspeople, a man and his lady carrying a holdall. They arrived with the driver leading the way. They were seated at the solitary wooden bench while the driver stood close by to interpret. The man pointed out that they couldn't stay long; they would be driven back to the Railway Hotel in Mosul to collect their luggage before boarding the night sleeper. They had already wasted a good part of the morning looking for the village; all they had to go by was a general description. The car hire driver did well to find it. They'd heard of another family who had come looking to acquire a girl for service. But no, they hadn't seen a girl by the name of Lamis, nor knew how she was.

Her mother brought Habiba close to where they were seated. With the help of the driver interpreting, the lady asked the girl her name and how old she was. The mother answered the questions. The lady looked straight at the girl, smiled benignly and commented on her long golden tresses, her freckles and blue eyes. She liked the name Habiba and wondered how they came by it, a "darling girl" in their language. The mother responded by saying her daughter was a good girl who did what she was asked to do, and without complaining.

The lady, addressing the girl, asked her how she had spent the morning. The mother answered, always through the driver interpreting, that her daughter was very hard working. As soon as she woke in the morning, she would go to the henhouse to collect the eggs, then come back to roll the mattresses, sweep the floor, then pick up the pail and go to the well.

"But she is so thin," observed the lady.

"She is a small eater," the mother replied. "Whatever I put in front of her, she doesn't finish it." Then she added hastily, "She isn't a fussy eater; she eats what we eat."

The husband stood up and walked to the door. They had driven for a long time in the mountains that morning and were going to do more that day, so he decided to go outside to stretch his legs. On the way out, he passed the father who had returned from the field. He saw his disposition and that he was now huddled on the doorstep, head bent down, eyes averted, expressionless. The man uttered some conventional words of greeting, to which the other nodded.

Inside, the lady unzipped her holdall and took out some ladies' garments that she had purchased especially for the occasion: a couple of under-dresses and puffy pants, a full-length gown adorned with beads, a gobarah belt made from metal coins in a chain, and a velveteen hat decorated with turquoise beads. The mother received the offering and gathered the clothing with unconcealed delight. She was particularly thrilled by the green gown, which she tried on for size. The lady then said she also had something for her daughter. She pulled out a floral dress and asked if she liked it and would like to try it on. Habiba nodded. Her mother told her to go to the inner room to change.

The lady said how pretty Habiba looked when she returned, while the mother observed that it wasn't a bad fit. The lady then said that it was all she had brought for the girl, but that she would take her shopping in town for whatever else was needed and fitted.

The man returned from his walk somewhat anxious about the time. He said they had to move on before darkness fell and then asked the women if they had finished their business. His wife said they had and started to rummage in her bag while the husband asked the driver to take the girl to the car and wait for them. The lady pulled out a plain silver bangle, which she gave to the mother who was overjoyed. She put it on, thanked the lady animatedly and instinctively went to hug her before catching herself in time.

The driver told Habiba not to worry as they made their way to the car. He said he had only met the couple that morning. They had come from the big city and were staying at the Railway Hotel, which was very expensive. They wanted a car with a driver for the day, and the management had recommended him. They seemed a nice, kindly couple – unlike some others he had come across. He guessed they were rich and must have a big house, perhaps with several servants. The girl mentioned her cousin Lamis when the driver mentioned others he had known, but he had no knowledge of her.

After the driver let her into the car, she crouched down and then sat up to have a last look. She saw the lady walking towards them; she wasn't carrying the holdall. Her father was standing, head bowed, next to the man. The man got out his wallet and pulled out a banknote, which he handed to her father. Her father bent down and kissed his hand. Her mother was walking back towards the cottage.

"Ummi," the girl called out in a low voice, which didn't carry much beyond the open window.

The mother walked over the doorstep and passed inside without a backward glance.

The girl was now overwhelmed by a dumb, bewildering sensation of primeval fear, longing, hope, expectation. She was no longer conscious of the man at the steering wheel in front of her, the lady walking up towards them, her father and the man of the wallet. Nor was she conscious of the henhouse from where she collected the eggs each morning, the goat tethered to the house next door that she milked for cheese-making in the afternoon, the people in the valley looking up, or the girls at the well.

Her eyes were fixed on the rough, uneven patch of ground in front of the cottage, the two hollowed stone steps, the door opening and the warm darkness beyond.

Nothing came out to break the darkness as the lady opened the car door to climb in.

"Ummi," the girl whispered again, before flopping down and curling herself up in the footwell.

* * *

The Man from Kirkuk

You can have your Baghdad, but do leave me my own. You can have your Rusafa, Karkh, Karrada and the riverbanks, but do leave me a spring's day, bright as the sun's rays shining on the throngs of people filling the markets, the tearooms and coffee houses bursting at the seams, and the long queue snaking along the pavement to the entrance of an imposing building.

It was the Ashura, season of pilgrimage to the shrines of the Imams, of devout pilgrims who, having handed their moneys to their banks in exchange for money drafts, were now queuing to cash them at the Baghdad branch of the Imperial Bank of Iran. Thus, the moneys were spared the plunder of the highwayman, only to be exposed to the wiles and depredations of the charlatan and pickpocket.

In the afternoon you would have seen me at al-Mutanabbi, a long covered street with a score of shops, each with a narrow frontage and deep interior, walls covered by shelves carrying books. I lingered at Hashim's and was offered an istikan of tea. He is my cousin and enquired after my father's health. When I asked about the business, he said it was quiet; of the many thousands of strangers in town that day very few spoke Arabic, and the diet of those few was other than the serious and antiquarian literature he had on offer.

I walked towards Hasan's and found Akram at work. He is a brilliant draughtsman and illustrator of book covers. His speciality is the Kufic calligraphy, but he would also use the cursive Diwani and al-Jazm as required. I saw him holding the thin sheet of paper flat on the palm of his left hand as he wielded the tracing pen with the other.

Moving further along I heard the collective clash of metal on metal, the sound becoming louder in time with the gradual lifting of the gloom as I reached the end of the street. I then emerged into bright sunlight and the deafening crescendo of a forest of hammers knocking the sheets of metal into shape as they fashioned all manner of domestic objects and utensils.

Halfway along the coppersmiths' market I turned into a narrow, poorly lit ginnel leading to a warehouse next to the derelict Mustansiriyya, founded in the thirteenth century as one of the world's oldest universities. I went through and came out onto a small quay by the fast-flowing Tigris; Ibrahim's tea shop a little distance beyond.

He filled me an istikan as I entered. He then whispered in my ear that we had a visitor and nodded in the direction of the man from Kirkuk.

I went to greet him. "Peace upon you."

"And upon you peace," he replied.

I sat next to him, put my istikan down and asked for a nargileh.

"We call it shisha," he said.

I could tell by his accent that he was not from our parts. I was keen to find out more, and to do so delicately and cautiously. He explained that he was from Kirkuk, and he was not Kurdish but a Turkuman. He said he was a clerk by occupation. I was particularly anxious to find out if he was in government service. He dispelled that notion by saying that he had been employed by a wool merchant and kept the accounts among other general duties. He did that for six years, then the merchant died and the business closed down leaving him unemployed. This remained the situation until he heard from his cousin who was working for a date wholesaler in Basra that there might be an opening for him in the same firm. He was now on his way. He had arrived on the Kirkuk train at midday and had four hours to kill before boarding the Basra train.

I wondered how he'd ended up at Ibrahim's tea shop, which had nothing special to commend it, being in a poor area and so out of the way. He said that at school he had heard of the golden age of Baghdad, of the House of Wisdom founded by al-Ma'mun and of the later foundation of the Mustansiriyya. He was hoping to visit the sites and accosted people in the street to ask for directions. He soon found out that there was no visible trace left of the former, while no one had heard of the latter, except an old man who thought it might be in this quarter.

I asked him how things were in Kirkuk, and he in turn asked how we were managing in Baghdad under the new government. We talked about the prices in the shops, the hardship suffered by all but the very rich and privileged, and we talked about the crowds. I told him to beware of the pickpockets.

I could see a little, almost imperceptible, bump where his breast pocket would be, but I kept quiet about that. He said he had been forewarned, told how evil and inventive the Baghdadi pickpockets were, only surpassed for wickedness and inventiveness by those of Mosul.

At hearing that, Abu Jasim, who was sitting in a corner by himself, evidently listening to our conversation, could not restrain himself. He exclaimed, as if to himself, "Nonsense, there is none more villainous than you would find here," and then took no further part in our conversation.

The visitor said that he saw no policeman as he walked about. I said the police were hopeless, many of them corrupt, almost all inefficient. Furthermore, they would have been instructed on a day such as this to maintain a low profile and avoid altercations and arrests. The thousands of annual pilgrims bring a lot of business with them; a pickpocket here and an overcharge or fraud there are a price worth paying. He said he could not understand why anyone would want to be a pickpocket. I said no one is born dishonest; it's circumstances that drive people to crime. He said he could not imagine anyone being so desperately poor that he would commit the most heinous crime of robbing a man who may have spent a whole year saving for a pilgrimage. I pointed out that in other countries the normal judgement was cutting off the thief's hand. I said I was in favour of that as a punishment and deterrent. He thought it too severe, that confiscation, imprisonment and exile would be enough punishment in most cases. He expounded that to apply sharia punishment in this regard was barbaric, that it was frowned upon even in the days of al-Ma'mun more than a thousand years before. That was before the clerical reaction set in under al-Mutawakkil. I was impressed by his erudition, and more so when he carried on expounding on the history of al-Mustansiriyya, its foundation by the progressive caliph al-Mustansir and its subsequent sack by the Mongol invaders.

I was enjoying our discussion, but it was brought to an abrupt end by the man looking at his watch and exclaiming anxiously that it was time for him to catch the train. After he stood, I laid down the nargileh and rose to walk with him to the street door. I thought the bump where his breast pocket would be was now a little more pronounced. As we came to settle up with Ibrahim, my companion raised his hand to his breast, but I held him back and called out "wayr", a Baghdadi expression intimating to the one in charge of the tearoom not to accept payment from a guest but to add the charge to one's own.

As soon as we got out we hurriedly bid "in Allah's safe keeping" each to each, and separated before he turned left and I right. I hurried along retracing my way back towards al-Mutanabbi Street.

I had good reason to hurry because as we were leaving the tearoom I managed to relieve the Kirkuk man of his money bag and transferred it to my cavernous pocket. I did that not without regret since I liked the man, and it may appear shameful to right-thinking people that I should treat him so, whom I befriended and treated as an honoured guest.

Back at Hashim's bookshop, I sat down and fished in my cavernous pocket. There was just the one money bag. It was my very own.

* * *

Abu Jasim

My name is Ahmad, but everyone calls me Abu Jasim. I am the leader of the Mustansiriyya lodge of the Baghdadi pickpockets. It goes by that name because our meeting place is Ibrahim's tea shop, being in a poor, neglected quarter of Baghdad, close to the derelict Mustansiriyya, which was founded in the thirteenth century as one of the world's oldest universities. Did I say leader? Correction, past leader! After the mortifying debacle that I sustained in Mosul, I stepped down from the leadership. In fact, my humiliation was so great that I gave up the profession altogether.

It all started when the man from Kirkuk came in off the street. He said he was a Turkuman from Kirkuk and gave us a cock and bull story. He said he was unemployed, on his way to Basra looking for a job as a clerk and that he chanced by our tea shop as he was looking for the university. I had my doubts about him from the very beginning. He was just too glib, too confident. He spoke with authority and exposed to view a good education, yet he was allegedly travelling the length of the country looking to be employed as a mere office clerk! At mention of pickpockets, he asserted that the cleverest and most inventive were the Mosulis. I was outraged and could not restrain myself; I said that there were none better than the Baghdadis. We know from what followed that the man was a true professional: he picked our brother Hammudi's pocket and took his money bag, which Hammudi got back by picking the other's pocket in turn. If you ask me, I would venture to suggest that the man was not from Kirkuk at all, but a Mosuli, one of Mosul's pickpocket fraternity, come specifically to cast down a challenge on us. Further, I guess he would have obtained information about us with the detail that our meeting place was a tearoom close to the Mustansiriyya, so he accosted people in the street asking for directions to the latter.

At our next lodge meeting, we discussed the matter under "Any Other Business". There was a feeling that we should pick up the gauntlet – not doing so would expose us to a lack of respect along with ridicule throughout Iraq and beyond. But some argued against that. Najib said it was uncertain whether saying the Mosulis were top notch, the man, allegedly from Kirkuk, had it in mind as a challenge, let alone expecting it to be seen by us as such. Hammudi recalled the words and the way they were uttered and that, in retrospect, after discovering the man was a pickpocket, he now felt quite certain that he was up to no good. That he meant to hurt, if not to challenge.

As the argument became heated, I pointed out that it mattered not what the man had intended; it was sufficient that the words belittling the Baghdadi pickpockets in general, and our lodge in particular, were likely to be repeated and spread as a rumour unless we put a stop to it. Haidar did not agree. That was always Haidar's way. Every time I expressed a view or suggested a particular course of action, you would find him contradicting and objecting. That may be due to his resentment at my election to the interim leadership of the lodge to last until brother Musa completed his spell in prison for committing an unfortunate blunder.

Haidar argued that it was unwise to rise to the bait; it would dignify the Mosulis, while we had nothing to gain. The Mosulis were nobodies, he observed, whereas our repute was worldwide. We can even boast several citations in *Thousand and One Nights.* What do they have to boast about? I dismissed Haidar's observation – to do otherwise would have been seen as weakness. But in retrospect, I wish I had acceded to his logic rather than allowing myself to be ruled by pride.

Eventually, after further discussion, it was resolved that one of us would go to Mosul to investigate and report. We budgeted for a return journey and one week's accommodation, the money to come out of the lodge's common fund. In doing so, we overruled Haidar's objection; he said it would be a waste of money, which we needed to conserve for the hard times that everyone was prophesising. Next was the question of who among us would undertake the trip. There were two or three willing to do it, even though it meant taking time off their normal work. There was even a suggestion that we determined the final choice by the drawing of lots. But I put an end to all that. The task was for me to undertake; I was the leader and would lead from the front.

I began to make preparations. I went to the draper's to be fitted with a jubbah to wear on top of the *thowb*. Mosul being a couple of degrees colder than Baghdad, I chose a double-lined one, open at the front from collar to waist and having two inside breast pockets. I then went to the coppersmiths' market where I had twelve discs cut into the precise size and shape of our gold lira. For money bags, I contrived two linen pouches with tapes. I put the fake liras into one of the pouches, thence to the left breast pocket; and the good spending money in the other pouch, thence to the other pocket. Before setting out, I made discreet enquiries and found out that the Mosuli pickpockets habitually frequented Ninawa, a coffee house in Makkawiyya.

When I arrived in Mosul, I found accommodation at Umm Raji's boarding house nearby. I went out the following morning, bought a newspaper and walked to Ninawa where I had a breakfast of Turkish coffee with clove, which was the house speciality, and an omelette ordered from the café across the road. I paid the man who brought it over out of the money bag I had in the right breast pocket. Then I remained inside the coffee house, observing the comings and goings while I had the newspaper spread out on the table in front of me.

A little time later a shoeshine boy arrived. I got the money bag out again, undid the string and paid him. Just before the midday call to prayer I got up, paid the house bill and left. I returned in the afternoon and sat at the same table. I called for a nargileh.

The waiter asked me, "What flavour?"

"A normal tobacco," I said.

"You are right," said the man at the next table. "One has to think of one's health."

"And to preserve one's senses," I added.

With the ice now broken, he got up and sat next to me. I introduced myself as a visitor from Baghdad. He asked how long I would be staying in Mosul. I explained that I intended to have a week's holiday in Shaqlawa and was also availing myself to the opportunity of spending a few days in his delightful ancient city. He said he knew Shaqlawa, a scenic hamlet in the mountain, good for relaxation and enjoyment with clear mountain air and free of midges at that time of year. The man from the café then came across and took orders for afternoon snacks. I ordered a cheese sandwich and paid for it out of the money bag. At first, I absent-mindedly half-pulled out the one in the left breast pocket. Immediately, I realised my mistake and pushed it back quickly and pulled out the other one.

At the end of the day, I returned to the boarding house where Umm Raji had prepared dinner for me. Later still I went to my room, performed the last of the day's five prayers, then undressed and went to bed. The money bags were intact.

The second day was a repeat of the first, even to the extent of partially pulling out the wrong money bag, immediately realising the mistake, pushing it back in, then getting out the other. Except that this time it was done deliberately!

The third day was a Friday, the best day for business. It is a social leveller, albeit the levelling lasting no more than a few hours: Merchant and landlord, expiating for short-changing and rent racking, would rub shoulders with you and me. They would bend down to remove the shoes, go genuflect for the *ruk'ats*, then come back to squat down to put on the shoes before emerging to a street packed with people.

In the afternoon, I saw the pickpockets arrive in Ninawa looking self-satisfied. They were now unwinding with tea in istikan, coffee in cup, "tobacco" in hookah, and snacks from across the road delivered with the bill by a serving youth, payment made with an expansive show of adding a generous tip. But what particularly caught my attention was a cocky youngster, face broken by a smile, talking animatedly to the one-eyed old man in the corner.

The young pickpocket got out a card and waved it around. "Look, look," he exclaimed, "this is the identity card of our chief of police, bearing his name, picture and his own signature as police chief next to the government seal!" He repeated that with glee while I felt disdain for what I judged to be youthful immaturity and incautious boasting.

As I heard him repeat the performance at the arrival of another customer, I could no longer contain the urge to knock him down a notch or two. "You would think it the mother of girls giving birth to a boy," I said, addressing my remark to the braggart.

"Meaning?" he retorted.

"I say enough of boasting. It is not so clever lifting the card from a policeman's back pocket in a crowded street on a Friday."

"For one thing it was the breast pocket, and who are you to tell me? What do you know about pickpocketing?"

"What I know is that I have been coming here these last three days with twelve gold liras in here," I said, tapping my left breast pocket, "and the money is still here intact."

Then it happened. The one-eyed old man in the corner broke into a full-throated laugh as he rose and came closer to engage me.

"My dear Baghdadi colleague and friend, did you think we would be taken in by your cock and bull story? Of coming to Mosul as a tourist to feast your eyes on our antiquities while spending all your days in this coffee house? We have worked it out that you are one of our Baghdadi brethren, come to spy on us. As regards the twelve gold liras that you claim to have in the money bag there in your left breast pocket, well…I assayed them three times with my needle, the last time not more than an hour ago and found they were brass."

As he finished those words, Ninawa rocked with laughter. I hurriedly stood up, left a banknote at the till and rushed out into the street, back to Umm Raji's and the railway station.

It was game, set and match to the Mosulis.

Now in retirement, I often recall my long misspent life, the triumphs and the defeats, the honour and the disgrace, and find myself reliving the great fall from grace in Mosul nearly every night in my dreams. I almost hear the mocking laughter and guffaws resounding in that accursed coffee house and the streets of Makkawiyya.

* * *

The Cull

He was shaken out of his midday torpor by the sound of a gunshot. He trembled as he heard the next one and saw the old grey come running away from its direction and past him without stopping. Then he saw the man with a rifle in the distance and remembered. He was overcome by terror, stood rooted to the spot – the same as it had been the other time. The dog cull on that other occasion was now a vague memory, but the terror and sadness, now reawakened, were raw. A young dog then, he did not know what was happening other than his mother standing between him and the man, he at her signal running away as fast as his delicate legs allowed, and not slackening when he heard the shot.

A defiant bark in the distance, a doleful shriek, and he unfroze and ran after the grey. Then as the grey turned right into the snicket, he had a different idea; he veered left to slide into a dry ditch at the side of the road. He dared not look behind while he hoped that he might be overlooked as he ran in the shadow of the bank. At the culvert he stopped, sweat dripping and breathless. He lay himself down, stretched, then gathered himself foetus-like in the cool womb-safe darkness. By and by, he recovered his breath, remembered the terror and experienced it anew as he felt the pounding of his heart.

He bounded out, sniffed the air, cocked his ears and looked about him suspiciously while pondering his next move. He set off cautiously towards Omar's teahouse where Tamata was the coffee boy. Tamata had started as a youth working for Omar's father. Now a frail old man, he was in charge of the coffee, which he carried in a beaked dalla as he served the customers.

In this cruel world of humans and dogs, Tamata was the only one who had shown him kindness. He would occasionally throw him a piece of stale bread or a dry date as he waited in the street, and there was one occasion when he allowed him inside the guardian's hut that was his home.

Tamata was not in the teahouse. He was in the hut, reclining on a mattress while resting from the stifling heat of the high summer at midday. A butt of a joint in his hand emitted a sickly smell. He had left the door open to let in fresh air. He was not pleased when he saw the dog steal in.

"What the devil! How can you have the nerve to barge in? You bastard! If I had not been resting, I would have got up to kick you out. Off with you, son of a whore! Was it not enough the bad luck you brought me last time? Have you come to add to my misfortune, you impure dog, son of many fathers? Yes, I know, I should blame myself. I should have remembered what I was told in the madrassah: Angels do not enter a house wherein is a dog. Did Gabriel not break his promise to Allah's Messenger? Kept himself outside because there was a dog in the house?"

The dog's nostrils flared. He turned his head to look at the open door, then turned back before crawling two small steps to bring him closer to where Tamata lay. He looked to him imploringly.

"What's the matter? What are you running away from? By Allah, you will not see me get up, nor move a finger to help you after what I suffered through you before. And when it is the time for prayer, I shall rise and expect you to get right out and not return. Was it not said that a prayer is annulled if a dog, a donkey or a woman pass in front of the prayer people?"

A gunshot was heard ominously close. The dog shivered. He slid a little closer to the mattress and looked at Tamata imploringly uttering a moan.

"Ah, so that's why. It has started, then. Lucky for you, you are not black. No one can deny the *hadith*. What is written is written. All dogs are impure; it were better if they did not exist. But that they are a species of creation. it would have been a duty to kill them. As it is, the black have to be killed. Allah's Apostle enjoined to kill in particular the jet-black dog having two spots on the eyes, for it is a shaytan."

The dog lifted himself on his forelegs, sniffed the air and cocked his ears. He uttered a moan, lay down and shook, eyes bulging, legs fluttering. He was having a fit.

"Never mind," said Tamata wistfully, "it wasn't your fault. How were you to know that in entering my home you were to bring me misfortune? I do not hold it against you. After all, I did let you in. There is no justice in this world. But one cannot question the *hadith*: Every time a man befriends a dog, Allah will dock a qirat of the man's heavenly reward for good deeds. I should have remembered that. Instead, I invited you in, befriended you, and what was my reward? A rash, then patches and pimples; some you can see even now. People looked at me and did not like what they saw. They avoided me; some regular customers stopped coming. I went to the mosque first, then Omar took me to the doctor's and sacked me. "*I cannot have a leper in my teahouse*", he said. The doctor said that with the medicine it would clear in six months. Omar said I could stay here until then, but not show my face. They bring me food to the door twice a day. No one wants to touch a leper."

The dog got up, moved to the door, sniffed, cocked his ears and stole out.

"What, you too! You unclean dog and son of a dog, bastard son of a whore and many fathers? By your black legs shall you be known. Tell me wherefrom did you get those black legs?"

The dog came back, a sammoon loaf in its mouth, which he put down next to Tamata.

"Ah, good boy. So that's why you went out! It was to steal a loaf to bring to me. How was I to know! No, don't push it towards me. You can't expect me to have it after it has been in your mouth. Did the Messenger of Allah not say that when a dog licks the utensil, you should wash it seven times and rub it with earth the eighth time? You see, I am not an ignorant, old fool. I had been to the madrassah as a boy and learnt well. Go on, you got the loaf and might as well eat it. It is no sin to steal bread when one is hungry. I shall not tell – we are brothers in our misery, aren't we? Unclean, untouchable? How wretched this life is! We are not punished for what we do; we are punished for what we are. Now, if I could be back at the madrassah, I would ask the master what was Allah's purpose in creating a specie and then wanting it destroyed? Ah, but I can imagine the answer: the master hitting me on the head with the cane and calling me an 'insolent kafir' for questioning Great Allah's design."

The dog gathered the sammoon in his teeth and turned his back on Tamata. He moved towards the door and squatted to take nibbles out of it ravenously. Then, all of a sudden, he dropped it and rushed back in, past the mattress, and cowered in the corner. A shadow blocked the entrance. A man holding a rifle.

"Is there a dog in there?" he called out.

"You have no business here," Tamata shouted back.

"I was told a dog was seen here."

Tamata lifted himself off the mattress. "I told you, you have no business here."

"It's only my job."

"And I suppose you enjoy it."

"I hate to do it."

"What have they done to you, the poor dogs?"

"We are only after the stray dogs."

"Well, you will not find any here."

Tamata stepped out of the shadow as he neared the opening and faced the gunman who looked at him and quickly turned away.

"It's the rabies, you know."

Tamata went back and lay himself down on the mattress. The dog approached; he patted him.

"Do not worry, little chestnut, nothing will happen to you. He has gone and will not want to come back. You are safe here with me. We are brothers, aren't we? Unclean, untouchable?

"Why, you are sniffling. Are you crying? Stop crying, you bastard. I have had enough of you. We are wretched, but it will pass. Soon the six months will be up. I shall then leave and go back to my village, and you will come with me. I shall seek out the sheikh and ask him to help me find work. Sheikh Ahmad will help; I am sure he will, even though he does not know me. He is head of the Habe tribe, and I shall remind him of my Habe family. I shall say I can be a guardian in an orchard. I would be content with a small wage. I shall ask him to overlook my age. I am a good worker, as is my dog, a good guard dog. You will be a good guard dog, won't you?

"What though you have black legs, it was clearly stated in the *hadith* that dogs are a nuisance, but the Messenger of Allah made an exception. He permitted the keeping of dogs to guard orchards and for the protection of cultivated land. So, stop sniffling, son of a bitch; I shall take you with me, away from here, to a new place, among new people. What though we are wretched, have nothing – that will pass. I shall get me a job, you will see, and you will help me, won't you? You owe it to me. We will manage, you will see – and Allah will provide."

❋ ❋ ❋

More Rejoicing in Heaven

Sam and Ben are first cousins. They live in the same street. Out of school they are a gang of two, engaged in all the games that boys of their age engage in, and more besides that are invented in the spur of the moment by Sam. Sam likes to lead, and Ben is content to follow. That is not simply because Sam is older, yet a year's difference is considerable when one is eight.

Ben's family is religious on the maternal side, grandfather as learned in the law as a *hakham*, and as strict in its observance as the *hakham bashi*. Ben goes to him every Saturday afternoon for an hour of bible reading and religious instruction.

As Sam's father is secular, he brought up his children to shun religious dogma and practices. Instead, to seek the truth through reason and to find moral instruction in the works of the world's great philosophers. Holding an office of profit in the community, he does not flaunt his secularism openly. On the Saturday, he would walk a few miles to join close friends and conspirators in some orchard or other lonely spot out of town where they would smoke unobserved.

On the eve of the Day of Atonement, he would attend the service. Every man has to do that, in the Great Synagogue, then return home after the *Kol Nidrei* to see that everyone in his household had a snack or drink so as to break any fast which may have been foolishly begun and pre-empt any that might be contemplated.

Friday evening is the start of the weekly pastime. The boys' fathers would spend it with men friends club-like in some coffee house in town or, as on this particular occasion, it being summer time, a tearoom on the edge of a date palm grove. Sam and Ben are taken along.

While the men sit down to exchange news and views while emptying one istikan of tea after another, the boys are left to their own devices, playing hide-and-seek, cowboys and Indians, the swordsman Zorro and Flash Gordon Conquering the Universe. Then as Flash sets out in pursuit, sweeping down in his spaceship to put to rout the army of Kala hiding in the bush, Ben stops suddenly and emits a shout as he sees it.

Hearing that, Sam comes riding through the encircling line of Indians to crouch next to Ben who excitedly points to the coin on the ground, a solitary fils.

"Stop, stop, don't touch it," cries Sam. "Don't do it, drop it. What would your grandad say if he saw you?"

Ben lets go the coin with a shaking hand.

"Have you forgotten?" adds Sam. "Did your grandad not tell you it's forbidden to handle money on the Sabbath?"

Ben now looks on the coin settled in the dust with suspicion and dismay. They then get up to resume their game; in an instant, the fils is in Sam's pocket.

They are now playing cops and robbers. Sam hides behind a palm tree. Ben goes to look for him. Sam is discovered.

"Stop, you are under arrest," Ben calls out.

Sam runs away and darts from one tree to another.

Ben's pursuit brings him to the bush. He looks for the coin but finds it's no longer there.

"Look, look, Sam. The fils is not there."

"Have you looked carefully?"

"Come and have a look, it's not there."

Sam comes near to have a look. "Yes, it has disappeared," he says. "It's a miracle."

"A miracle?"

"Yes, a miracle. Did your grandad not tell you about miracles? Allah has taken the fils away because it is the Sabbath," Sam concludes.

Ben is satisfied. He always believes what Sam tells him.

The street boy vendor arrives with his tray of sweetmeats. He is not much older than Sam. Every day he goes about selling the home-made confections. They are not the same every day. The boys rush towards him to see what he has. It is simsim, sticks of sesame in treacle. He tells them it's two fils the stick, nothing else, nothing cheaper. Sam asks if he would let them have half a stick for one fils. He says not, for who will be there to buy the other broken half.

The boys walk away disappointed. Then Sam has an idea. He asks Ben if he likes simsim, and Ben nods. Sam then tells Ben to get a fils from his father to be added to the one that he will get from his. They would then buy a stick, which they would share. Ben agrees as he always does to Sam's ideas and suggestions.

Ben goes to speak to his father and gets the fils. Sam goes to where his father is sitting conversing with others. He pretends he was asking, but does not. He rejoins Ben who gives him the fils, which he adds to the one in his pocket.

The street vendor is still there, so Sam gives him the two fils and chooses one of the sticks. He breaks it in half, gives one half to Ben and pockets the other. While Ben starts to bite, crunch and chew his half-simsim with undisguised pleasure, Sam is in no hurry to do so. It's always so with Sam. He savours the possession of the sweetmeat and the anticipated pleasure before its consummation.

As Ben finishes his simsim, Sam gets out his half-stick. He is smug, feels superior. Ben has had his simsim and is now empty-handed; but he, Sam, still has his along with the anticipated pleasure of biting, crunching and chewing.

Ben now looks wistfully at Sam and longingly on the half-stick in his hand. Sam knows that feeling. Then, as if seeing his young cousin and playmate in a new light for the first time that evening, a strange new sensation rises and stirs within him, enveloping him in its grip.

He lifts the half-stick to his mouth, takes a nibble and hands the rest to his friend. Ben receives it with appreciation and relish, while in his grandad's heaven they look on and rejoice.

❊ ❊ ❊

A Singer in the Court of Harun al-Rashid

My name is Mukhariq. I was brought up in humble circumstances, such that I could not hope for any better; for how could I look forward to anything better, being the son of a poor butcher, one of the poorest butchers of Kufa. My father did not own the shop, the goods or anything within it. He himself was owned by his master who had bought him in the slave market and set him up to slaughter the sheep, cattle and camels that he would then sell.

From the moment I was born I, being my father's son, was also the master's property. He was an eminent man. People were in awe of him, respecting his great wealth, the number of his slaves and freedmen, as well as the influence he wielded, being closely related to the governor. He was strict in the way he treated his slaves, so my poor father could never slacken.

I grew up helping my father in the business. When I was ten years old, I discovered, the same as others discovered, that I had an exceptionally good voice; so my father told me to use it to market the meats. I would stand in the street by the shop's entrance to shout enticing spiels, modulated and tuneful, to laud the freshness and wholesomeness of what we were offering. I did that day after day and by and by we acquired regular customers who would come especially to listen to me and make a purchase, or just to listen.

The master had a good eye for business. When he learnt about my voice and its effect on customers, he took me to an eminent singer of Kufa and asked her to instruct me in the finer aspects of singing and lute playing. But as soon as she heard me, she was so enthralled by the quality of my voice that she bought me on the spot. Thereafter, she instructed me so assiduously that in time I learnt all that she knew of the art of singing and lute playing, which was yet limited as I later discovered.

One day, I was to put on a fine new suit and she took me to Baghdad. At the slave market, we were accosted by an agent who made his living by introducing the superior quality slaves to private buyers; he would earn a commission if the introduction resulted in a deal. He judged that my voice, singing and lute playing were so superior that, added to my acuity, placed me above being auctioned or offered for sale publicly in the market place. He said I was more suited to be offered to the most discerning of high society. He brought us to none other than the great Ibrahim al-Mawsili, doyen of the singers and instrumentalists of Baghdad and consort of caliphs and aristocrats.

After Ibrahim listened to my singing, he asked the woman, "How many dirhams do you hope to gain by selling this lad?"

She pondered the question and, with due regard to the usual protracted haggling that would ensue, came up with what she thought was an exaggerated price for a start. "Ten thousand!"

Ibrahim laughed and said without a moment's hesitation, "Done, you have a deal, he is worth more."

The woman, repenting her offer, was sorely vexed. She alleged it had been a mistake and begged Ibrahim not to hold her to the bargain while insisting at the same time, "I could not have let him go for less than twenty thousand."

"Agreed," he said mockingly. "He is mine for twenty thousand, and he is still worth more."

The woman cried out in anguish. She said that she reposed her trust in Ibrahim al-Mawsili's universally acknowledged generosity and goodness of heart that would not suffer him to take advantage of a poor, simple, ignorant provincial woman newly arrived from Kufa. "Make it thirty thousand and I shall not ask for more."

Ibrahim now added to her anguish. "He is mine for thirty thousand dirhams, and he would still be worth more."

The woman was now beyond herself in anguish. She trembled and went red in the face, but she fell on his hand and confirmed the bargain. He said he would send her the thirty thousand dirhams with three thousand added to pay the agent.

I learnt a great deal about all aspects of music after I came into the ownership of Ibrahim al-Mawsili and was enrolled in what was in effect a music academy maintained by him and his genius of a son, Ishaq. I then realised that what I had managed to learn from the Kufan woman was but a drop in the great ocean of music, while the Mawsilis father and son practised in a boundless sea. So I immersed myself in it and garnered priceless artistic pearls exceeding what the others of the craft could boast of possessing.

Then it so happened that my master Ibrahim took me along to the grand vizier al-Fadl al-Barmaki. After listening to my singing, al-Fadl asked my master if he would sell me. My master replied truthfully and proudly that while I had cost him thirty-three thousand dirhams, he would not let al-Fadl have me for less than thirty-three thousand dinars. Al-Fadl recoiled at that figure which would leave Ibrahim with a massive profit; he said I was nowhere worth such a price. I was sore unhappy to hear the denigration and my master saw it as an insult. He said there could not be anyone in the whole world who had a singing voice to compare with mine. He then added proudly and defiantly as a final shot, "I would make you a gift of this lad rather than rebate the price."

"I accept him as a gift," said al-Fadl with a smile. As grand vizier, he was accustomed to give as well as receive gifts from friends, well-wishers, ambassadors and petitioners.

News of me reached Harun a-Rashid. When Ibrahim al-Mawsili attended one of his regular musical sittings, al-Rashid engaged him. "O Abu Ishaq, what's this I heard about the lad that you gifted to al-Fadl?"

"And what a lad," replied al-Mawsili. "There's no better singing voice in the whole of humanity, be they Arabs or aliens."

"How much is he worth?"

"The tribute of Egypt; nay, Egypt itself."

"Woe to you, Ibrahim. Do you know what you are saying? Can any singer be worth that much?"

"How can one put in the scales all that's of material value as counterweight to a singing voice that's unique?"

I passed on from the ownership of vizier al-Fadl to the Commander of the Faithful, Harun al-Rashid. On the first occasion that I appeared in the khalifal musical sitting, I sang standing on my feet. To sing standing reflected the lower status of the singers, while the more exalted leaders of the craft performed while seated.

Al-Rashid was so captivated by the quality of my singing that he motioned to me after I had rendered a few songs. "Mukhariq, go and sit with your peers, for you are above them who sing standing."

He followed that by awarding me three thousand dinars, which was the kind of big award that only those who had sung for him for at least ten years aspired to receive.

On the following musical sitting, I sang the following while seated:

"O, house of Salma, you have stirred my emotions,
a home whose denizens are no more.
Replaced by none
but the wild boar
Roaming in wasteland
wilderness under the stars."

This caused al-Rashid to break into tears. As I finished, he cried out, "Well done, Mukhariq. How shall I reward you?"

I hastened with a reply, lest the mood changed and the propitious opportunity was lost. "My wish, O Commander of the Faithful, is that you set me free from bondage. And that Allah may reward you and set you free from all ills."

"You are free," he said. "Repeat the song as a free man."

I repeated the song, which again caused the caliph's eyes to well.

He lifted the cup to his lips and said, "Well done, Mukhariq. Tell me what else you want me to give you as a reward?"

"The income of an estate for me to have for a living, and to include a house with furniture and servants."

Al-Rashid ordered that I received all those things. He then summoned his army chief Harthama who arrived dragging a heavy sword. He said to him, "O Harthama, do you recall a kharijite by the name of Mukhariq that we killed in Mosul? What was his nickname?"

"His nickname was Abu l-Mihna," the General recalled on the spot.

"You may leave," rejoined al-Rahid.

Harthama left. As a military man he could attend military sittings or counsels of war, but it was forbidden for him to attend the caliphal musical sittings.

Al-Rashid then turned to me. "I am naming you Abu l-Mihna, 'The Artist', in acknowledgement of your professionalism. And I am also awarding you one hundred thousand dirhams."

My reputation as a singer grew apace, and so did the respect and social standing that accompanied it.

One day, the celebrated poet Abu l-Atahiya came knocking on my door. He held himself out to be austere and ascetic. In reality he was worldly, his house full of gifts that he received as well as the money awards of which he spent but little.

He sat himself down at ease on the cushions with his legs crossed. He began to flatter me by saying that I was the best singer in Iraq, and further addressed me as the physician of the land of Babylon – my singing a balm to broken hearts. He followed this by entreating me to pour some singing into his ears, for it may gladden his heart and revive his spirit.

He later added on the same theme, "Your singing is a cure to madness. So smooth that were it liquid, I would have imbibed it as the water of life."

Shortly after he left my house, it occurred to me that he might not have long to live and so I might not see him again. Exercised by that sombre thought, I betook myself to his house and found him sitting in an earthen circular bath, stark naked, water up to his waist, so all I could see were his torso and his knees breaking the surface.

Seeing him thus, I could not contain myself laughing and said to him, "Woe to you, Abu l-Atahiya. What have you done to yourself?"

He became tearful and said, "By Allah, one does not need more in this life; yet foolish folk seek out more."

I said to him reproachfully, "Would you stretch that notion to the extent of your casting off the very clothes that covered your nakedness, which Allah does not exact? You should remember the ascetic folk wear the silk in Paradise, and that nakedness is not a religious duty in this world or the next."

Those words of mine appeared to have embarrassed Abu l-Atahiya. He asked me to retire to another room so he could dress. After a while, and with him now fully clothed, we sat down and he called for food and drink. I swallowed a few bites and took even fewer sips as he attended to the platter, greedily clearing the lot. Then, as if for a dessert, he asked me to sing the following song, the verses being of his own composition:

"*The mention of me will be shunned,*
and friendship forgot.
And to the bosom friend after me,
will be a bosom friend.
If my spell in this epoch is ended,
then the keening of the women mourners is of no avail."

When I finished, he sobbed to the extent of wetting his beard. He said, "Should my people send for you when I am at death's door, do not tarry to come along to be near to me; it will be my last wish that you came to sing those verses in my ear as I breathed my last."

I felt very sorry for this man who, in the decrepitude of old age, had turned to a mix of asceticism and worldliness, disdain of human affectation and a death wish.

I am now seventy years old, yet my singing voice is still the same as what enchanted people for a full fifty years, starting in the caliphate of al-Rashid and right up to that of al-Mutawakkil. Thus, it so happened that I sang for six caliphs in succession and for countless princes, viziers and aristocrats. That made me one of the richest men of Baghdad, gaining and amassing so much that I could have paid for one hundred thousand shops like the butcher's shop in which I started if I had wanted. I would add that I do not eat the meat.

Yesterday, a soothsayer warned me not to consume the cold foods. He prophesised that I will die of eating a cold cauliflower. But by now, and at my age, life itself has turned cold; so let my end come as it is willed, hot or cold.

* * *

The Minaret

The Bab al-Sheikh that I knew was a plebeian district of Baghdad that lay at a deferential distance from the main thoroughfares of stores, boutiques, refined restaurants and grand hotels. The inhabitants comprised of artisans, small traders, humble employees in straitened circumstances and, poorest of the poor, the *kasiba* who had no regular employment but sought a precarious livelihood by doing odd jobs as and when required. The area was also a labyrinth of congested humanity. There were dark, narrow streets that turned to rivers of mud when it rained, old houses in multiple occupation with flat roofs level with each other and separated by low walls – ideal as a getaway for lawless people to hole up, as well as for the political activists and their underground presses.

It is also an old historical district close to what was the site of the Abbasid Palace on the Rusafa side of Baghdad. That is also reflected in the name "Sheikh", which refers to Abdul Qadir al-Gaylani, leading jurist and Sufi head who died in 1166 and whose shrine is in the Bab al-Sheikh bearing his name.

Shrine and palace did not survive internecine civil wars and invasions. The shrine was destroyed by the Safavids and rebuilt by the Ottomans in the sixteenth century, while the site of what was the mosque of the caliphs became Suq al-Ghazl (yarn market). A once thriving textile industry that in its heyday counted a good number of handloom weavers, it went into a terminal decline after the British occupation of Iraq in the First World War followed by unequal competition from the Lancashire mills.

While the name survived, the area took another turn and became a thriving market for the sale of domestic animals – pigeons, in particular. Racing, or rather city sporting, pigeons were ever popular for sport. They provided one of the few pastimes for city dwellers, flying them in flocks off the roofs of houses. The choicest were very valuable, up to five hundred dinars for one pigeon according to a ninth century report! The main point of the sport is to inveigle some pigeons belonging to a rival flock to break ranks in flight and join one's own flock.

This innocent pastime had its detractors. They looked down on those engaged as idle good-for-nothings who had nothing better to do than spend their days on the roofs in full sight view of the women in the yards of neighbouring houses, and miss the right times for prayer. It was often sufficient to identify a potential witness in court as a rooftop pigeon fancier and for his testimony to be excluded on the grounds of unreliability.

Besides the pigeons, also on sale were doves, songbirds, parrots, swans, cats, chicken, gazelles and monkeys; squirrels, guinea pigs, gerbils and the occasional peacock; maize and other animal feeds; and rose water and other perfumes. And for Eid al-Adha, there would be many sacrificial sheep and fewer goats to be acquired by the well-to-do, who would take them to be ritually slaughtered and then shared among family, friends and the poor, each getting a one-third share.

A notable still-standing vestige of the glory days of Abbasid Baghdad is the Minaret of Suq al-Ghazl, which was constructed to form part of *Jami' al-khulafa'* (mosque of the caliphs). There is a story about the circumstances of its construction that has passed down through the generations and in the process undergone, as with all oral traditions, several changes of detail while retaining the core theme. In fact, the same core theme can be seen at the heart of other stories in diverse cultures, original themes being but a few in number. It is the story of two men and a minaret.

There is a popular saying that in the sum total of civilisation, Persia contributed chess, the lute and polo; from Greece came geometry, medicine and astronomy; and the Arab genius lay in grammar, jurisprudence and poetry. To that last, one should add architecture.

He was born in the Persian city of Ahwaz of an Arab father and Persian mother. He left home in his teens and went to seek his fortune in Baghdad. He did well as an architect and builder, in time becoming a master builder, then acknowledged as the master of all the master builders. His speciality was the building of minarets, for which his reputation spread far and wide, while his services as planner, architect and builder were in demand for major public works and private projects. He would receive commissions from as far afield as Basra and Samarra, for which he would be rewarded handsomely. He remained a bachelor, explaining, if asked indelicately, that he was so busy in his business that he had no time for a wife or family.

But as the business became established, and its demands grew, he betook himself to the slave market and bought a Circassian youth to serve him as general helper and apprentice. He treated him kindly, giving him to eat what he ate and be clothed with what he wore, in time regarding him as the son he never had. He taught him all that there was to learn in the craft, while the slave, being a keen learner, readily took note of all that he saw and heard, absorbing lessons and experiences that were expanded by an acute intellect. He reciprocated the master's kindness and concern with hard work, devotion and respect.

They were in Kufa at the preliminary stage of constructing a minaret when the caliph call arrived requiring the master builder to attend upon him to discuss an important project that he had in mind. Responding to the call, the builder made his way to Baghdad, leaving it to his slave to take care of the Kufa project in his absence.

As he came up before the caliph, the latter told him that he had planned to have a new mosque built close to the palace and wanted him to design and oversee the construction of a suitable minaret. The builder said that he could not attend to that for the next two years given his other commitments. The caliph was displeased. The builder explained that having accepted the commission for the Kufa mosque and received a down payment followed by his drawing up of the plans, setting a budget, ordering the materials and employing the masons, he was morally bound, no less than contractually, to remain in Kufa and oversee the project's completion by the agreed delivery date. As that failed to mollify the caliph, the builder suggested that the commission be given to his man, young in years but wise in experience and knowledge, who over the years had been his pupil and assistant and knew as much about minarets as he himself. The caliph was not fully mollified. He was particularly exercised by the thought that the minaret of what was to be the mosque of the Abbasid caliphs be constructed by a mere slave, and how that fact might be regarded by his subjects. The builder assured the caliph that whoever was commissioned to build the minaret at his recommendation would assuredly be a free man.

The master builder returned to Kufa and gave a report to his slave of what had transpired between him and the caliph. The slave was startled, covered in confusion, not knowing how to respond, tongue-tied while listening to the words that his master addressed to him.

"Son – and to me, you are like a son – the commission to build a minaret in the mosque of the caliphs is an important business, prestigious no less than profitable. I could not accept the commission, nor did I want it to knock on doors other than ours. So I suggested that it be given to you. The Commander of the Faithful was sufficiently persuaded to require you to attend before him to discuss the project and at the same time satisfy him of your suitability. This is a once in a lifetime opportunity for a young man like you. What's more, the caliph was unhappy that the builder of the minaret of his mosque be a foreign slave. So, from this moment I grant you your freedom so that you might go to Baghdad to carry out the project as a free man, and that with Allah's blessing it may be the start of a successful career all of your own."

The slave, while thanking his master for releasing him from bondage, said that he had been as happy while his master's slave as any free man in Baghdad. He added that he would go before the caliph and undertake the commission as his master's freedman and for his master's account.

The master dismissed the suggestion. "I am an old man coming to the end of my working life. It is now your turn to have your own business, establish your own reputation, make money, marry and, unlike me, have the blessing of a family and sons who will carry your seeds and bear your name."

The slave said that if he did build the minaret, he would share the benefit with his master who, besides being his master and teacher, would have been instrumental in his being given the commission.

The master again brushed that aside. "I am neither indigent nor mean as to want to share in the good fortune and rewards of another man's labour. You keep all the moneys and awards, and may Allah's blessing be in them for you."

Just as the slave, now a freedman, was taking his leave to depart to Baghdad, the master wished him a safe journey and that good fortune be ever his companion. He then added, "The one thing I wish for is that were you to receive the commission from the caliph, you would then address yourself to the task of building the minaret with the diligence I know you are capable of and do all you can to produce a minaret fit for kings. I do not need to point out that were you to fail in that respect, it would not only be bad for your prospects but also cast a shadow on my reputation, given that everyone knows I have been your guide and mentor over the years."

The slave said that he regarded his master's reputation precious above all else, adding, "I would rather die than you suffer any embarrassment on my account. You may rely on me. I shall not let you down."

Time passed, the mosque of the caliphs was completed and graced by the minaret built by the freedman. In the meantime, his erstwhile master had finished the minaret in Kufa followed by another project in Basra before returning to Baghdad.

The freedman was overjoyed to greet him, and impatient to show him his minaret and to boast of it as the culmination of his diligence and the fruit of all that he had learnt as a slave. "You see, I did not let you down," he said as they approached the minaret. With an open hand and extended arm, he proudly invited his former master to view it.

The latter felt the view as a dagger to his heart. What he saw in front of his eyes was a marvel of a minaret, better than any he had ever seen, better than any he had ever built, far superior to the one he had finished in Kufa, which was the cause of his declining the caliph's commission in the first place.

The freedman, in his excitement, was oblivious to the older man's visible signs of anger and torment – the blood draining from his face, the perspiration, the bulging eyes, the frozen face muscles, the hands made as fists.

The freedman was pleased with himself as he pointed to his extensive use of the muqarnasat to support the enclosed passageway and circular gallery, the arabesque-carved brickwork and geometric patterns. But every time he referred to his minaret, his style, his innovations, the older man felt it as a painful blow. His inner voice protested and screamed silently, *this should have been my achievement, by right my minaret, the fruit of a commission that had been offered to me first, which I foolishly declined, thus allowing it to be picked up by my underling, a Circassian of unknown parentage that I picked up in the slave market and nurtured over the years.*

He recalled an ancient saying that fitted the situation: I taught him archery every day but as soon as his arms grew steady and strong, he shot me. He was inwardly seething as he saw the twelve-sided base. He could not contain himself and said, "I know of no other twelve-sided minaret base. Where did you get the idea?"

"You are right; there is no other like it in the whole of Iraq. It was my own idea that came to me one day. Do you like it?"

"Do I like it? I hate it. I hate the muqarnasat. I hate the minaret. I hate you for causing me this embarrassment."

"Embarrassment? Do you see anything wrong?"

"No, I see nothing wrong. I see a perfect minaret devised in a manner which people will say is better than anything I have ever devised and built."

"I shall dedicate it to you as my master and mentor. I shall engrave the words on the bricks so they be there at all times to be read by whomsoever shall stand to cast an eye over my minaret."

"And, no doubt, people will think it magnanimous of you, a young man condescending to acknowledge a debt to an old man whom you supplanted. The commissions will now fly to your door."

"Nay, treat my door as yours. Whatever comes to me, I will share with you. Better still, there is some talk of a new mosque in Haidariyya, and I have been asked if I was interested in building the minaret. I shall ask them to give the commission to you instead."

"Am I hearing correctly? My slave, Circassian slave, a nobody that I picked in the slave market, is now my benefactor? My patron? Do you have the temerity of imagining that I would put up with such disgrace?"

"No, no, as Allah is my witness, I shall forever think of myself as your slave who basked in your goodness."

"No, by Allah, I see before me a traitor who is shaming me. One who had vowed to kill himself were he to cause me hurt or embarrassment."

"I pray to Allah to give you a long life as I absolve myself from ever wanting to cause you harm."

"Traitor, the harm is this thing that you created while I was away. The embarrassment is you standing at its entrance preening yourself."

At this point, the older man, master builder, seething with rage, lost all control. He picked up a hammer lying on the floor and hit the brick wall as if to demolish the accursed minaret. He then wheeled around and with a piercing cry of "Traitor, you deserve to die!" raised the hammer over the freedman's head.

The latter retreated inside the minaret and ran up the stairs followed by his master holding the hammer in hot pursuit. He was not as fit and fleet of foot as the younger man, but he would catch up with him at the top; that's where the accounts would be settled.

But as the older man reached the top of the stairs and the muezzin's gallery, there was no sign of the younger man. Another innovative feature that the latter had devised was to add a second gallery so that a passage ran from the main gallery to the other, which then connected to and emerged onto the staircase further down.

This was the last straw. The old master builder, once acknowledged as the master of all the master builders of Baghdad, now saw that his erstwhile slave had made good his escape. He accepted that his genius made him a better architect and master builder than himself. It was more than he could bear. With a heart-rending scream, he climbed the balustrade and flung himself to his death.

As a crowd gathered around the broken body at the foot of the minaret of Suq al-Ghazl, the freedman could be seen standing a few paces away crying and cursing his minaret, which he vowed would be his last.

❊ ❊ ❊

An Old Man's Advice

HKM is the etymological foundation of a constellation of words in Classical Arabic broadly denoting restraint, control, governance; and by extension *hakīm* (learned man, physician), *hākim* (ruler) and *hakhām* (rabbi).

Son, you will soon be making your own way in the world, living for a time with people not your own. I shall now give you the very same advice that as a young man, about your age, I received from a wise old man. You will achieve successes and feel proud, make mistakes and regret them; you will come by all kinds of situations and all manners of people: the good and the bad, the straight and the cynical, the benign and the malignant, the friend and the adversary. My one advice is to beware the friendships of three persons: the *hakīm*, the *hākim* and the *hakhām*. That surprises you, does it not? So, let me explain.

I once had a friend, a very good friend. We were mates at primary school and then at high school. He was a brilliant scholar, went to medical school and qualified as a doctor. I was less so and joined the family's haberdashery business, but we continued to be good friends.

Whenever anyone in the family fell ill, my friend the *hakīm* was generous with his professionalism, time and care. He was my best man when I got married and we saw a lot of him as a regular visitor afterwards. When we had our first child, we named him Simon, after him.

It was a hot summer and illnesses were rife. My wife observed that the child had a temperature. My friend said it was a summer indisposition and would pass. But the child did not get better; the potions that were prescribed did not appear to help. My wife kept urging me to employ another *hakīm* as a replacement or to have the benefit of a second opinion. I resisted that because I had faith in my friend and did not want the embarrassment of showing that we might have lost confidence in his ability, which he would take amiss. That was a fatal error. By wanting to keep the friendship of the *hakīm* we lost the friendship and the child.

Now, let me tell you about *hākim*. No, I do not say avoid rulers; that you cannot do anyway. Nor do I say avoid their friendship altogether. My advice is to be cautious when they befriend you.

A wise man who lived in Italy ages ago summed it up well: put not your trust in princes.

Nearer home, the story of the rise and fall of the Barmakis is a good illustration. They were a family of high officials of Persian ancestry, wielding great power and influence in the court of Harun al-Rashid. They were celebrated, their name a byword for liberality and munificence, such that even today we call a man "Barmaki" to describe a generous patron. The family played a big part in raising Harun to the caliphate. When he was growing up, Yahya al-Barmaki was officially his secretary, unofficially his guardian. He grew up benefiting from the support and protection of the Barmaki family. At times, he would address Yahya as "Father".

Upon his accession, he chose Yahya to be his vizier. Yahya and his four sons then rose to be the moving force of the caliphate, with the government administration including the Treasury in their hands. They were respected as much for their virtue, ability and liberality as for the power they exerted. And anyone who bore the name Barmaki basked in their glory.

When Yahya retired, his son al-Fadl succeeded him as chief vizier. State business apart, Harun and al-Fadl were particularly close, their friendship went back to the time when as callow youths they grew up together as almost of the same family.

It so happened that one day they went as caliph and vizier to visit the estate of a nobleman who was also a Barmaki. After the meal, the two guests went out for a stroll in the orchard, holding hands and admiring the scenery. They came by a cluster of pomegranate trees and one particular fruit on a hanging branch caught the eye of al-Fadl. He stretched himself to his full height but could not quite reach it. Harun bent forward and suggested that al-Fadl climb onto his shoulders to pick it, rejecting al-Fadl's protestation and the suggestion that the caliph should climb over the vizier. And that was how it was settled. Al-Fadl climbed over the shoulders of Harun and possessed the fruit. The landowner observed the scene from afar.

When it was time to take their leave, the caliph asked the landowner how he wished to be rewarded for his hospitality. The man replied, to the surprise and dismay of caliph and vizier, that all he wanted was for it to be acknowledged and accepted from that moment and forever that he was renouncing his Barmaki connection and lineage.

Time passed and the historical fall of the Barmakis occurred. The caliph had the whole family invited to a banquet and, so it is said, they were, with a few exceptions, massacred at midnight in cold blood. Yahya and al-Fadl were to die in prison. No reason was ever assigned for those dramatic events.

Over the years, there have been many theories advanced including *harem* intrigue speculations. All those who bore the name Barmaki were devastated. Some paid with their lives, others with their liberty, all with their wealth.

When the caliph's agents came to the nobleman landowner, he claimed that, contrary to their information, he was not a Barmaki. At his insistence, he was brought before the caliph and he reminded the caliph of the visit, the renunciation and its acknowledgement. The caliph asked him what had been in his mind at the time he made the renunciation. He said that in the first place he felt unhappy to see the caliph humbling himself, but far more than that he was struck by the great love the caliph and vizier had for each other, and it occurred to him that with such a great love the very gates of hell would open were they to fall out. It is said that on hearing those words, the caliph's eyes welled as he was visited by gnawing remorse.

Son, what shall I now tell you about *hakhām*? The clerics, with few exceptions, are troublemakers. They incite their flock against other faiths. They conspire against each other. They are most worldly even as they sermonise. They creep and crawl for their bellies' sake from a rich man's reception to a rich man's banquet. They preach faith but cannot keep faith with anyone. I speak from bitter experience.

Do you remember Rabbi Ezra? No? He was before your time. He was a sort of friend. Our door was ever open to receive him. He would call at my house to give religious instruction to my daughters. He officiated at the wedding of the eldest. He would call at my warehouse whenever he wanted to raise money for some community project or another. He was clever and learned in the law; one grants him that. So when the position of *hakham bashi* fell vacant, he threw his hat, or I should say turban, into the ring. He represented the hard wing of the rabbinate, his adversary the more moderate. I supported the latter, who prevailed.

Rabbi Ezra took the defeat very badly. He talked of cabals. He alleged he was the victim of secret deals and conspiracies. He told anyone who would listen that I did not keep a kosher house, and that he could testify from his own personal observation and experience that we used the same utensils for the meat and the milk. Do I need to say more?

* * *

The Examination

"Do take a seat. This will not take long. Just a few questions. Silly questions. I would not mind telling you, between you, me and the doorpost, that whoever devised them had no idea what for. You want to go to France, you are required to obtain a security clearance, you are referred to me and I have to ask stupid questions. You would think a security clearance would be needed for those arriving, not for those who are leaving.

"I have to ask you first of all if you are a member of the Communist Party. Now, before you answer that question, I have to warn you that whatever you say may be noted down and used in evidence. That is a legal requirement we often forget, if you know what I mean. The stupidity of it! Requiring a detective to question a suspect and to advise him not to answer. Now, in your case, I know what your answer would be, so I note it down, that is if you have no objection: I am not and have never been a member of the Communist Party.

"You know, from the moment I read *al-Ayyam* I have dreamt of going to France to study and experience life there as Taha Hussain described it. That unfortunately is an impossible dream in my case. Instead, I am here in this job – and do you think I like it? Still, it is better than being a bus inspector. I would give an arm and a leg to be able to give up all this and go abroad to study, be able to go to Paris as in your case, or just abroad as in Akram's case.

"Are you going to meet Akram? You don't have to tell me if you don't want to. Besides, I do have a copy of a letter here with a Beirut postmark. When did you last see Akram? You know what I mean, here in Baghdad before he slipped out and got away.

"I see you want to go to France to study medicine and return fully qualified. What can be nobler than that! I take it you would eventually want to return. After all, you have everything here: your country, your home, your family. Akram also has his family, but he may not venture to return, fearing he would be arrested or rather rearrested if he did. Is that not so? He told you as much in his letter. Or is he hoping, ever the optimist, that, let us say, things may take another turn? It was stupid of him to divulge so much, relying on security using an unsophisticated, I would say fairly transparent, use of pseudonyms. Do you not agree? Or is it a case of adolescent bravado, calling the party leader *hajji* and referring to the Syrian one as the professor? And then there is the mysterious one referred to as mukhtar!

"Have I just said something that troubled you? I would offer you a cigarette, but I have given up smoking. There was a time when I found it soothing, particularly when I was troubled. Was that also your experience? I am troubled a lot in this job, but mostly through minor instances. Right now, I am troubled by the reference to *mukhtar.* Who do you suppose that could be?

"So, you gave up smoking as well! That's amazing; it shows a high degree of self-control. You were a heavy smoker once. The last time I saw you, you were chain-smoking. That's right, I did see you; that was the second time. You did not see me. It is always so with me. People do not see me, or they see but do not recognise me. There were so many of us. There would have been many more if the gathering was better advertised and the venue not so far away. That was Akram's idea, to have the meeting at Salman Pak by Khosroe's Arch, or it could have been decided by others higher up in the party. The meeting was meant to lay the foundation stone for the first national students union; they must have miscalculated that Salman Pak would be beyond the authorities' prying eyes.

"Do you think Akram can be persuaded to return? He may wish it in his heart of hearts as he wastes his days, making hardly any impression, while causing embarrassment by wild talk of human rights, opposition to the regime coupled with a well-publicised fear of assassination, which, of course, is baseless. Certainly, there would need to be a discussion about the terms. And one cannot ignore the blameless warder who was injured as he got in the way, a serious flesh wound; fortunately, not life threatening. The wonder is how Akram came to have the knife!

"It was Akram who nominated you as secretary. You were one of only three members of the National Democrats at Salman Pak. You happened to quote from an article in *Liberation.* That went down well with the comrades. Akram said it would be good to have someone who could correspond with the outside world in French and English, and there was no dissent. A crafty move was that, to enable them to claim that the proposed leadership was not entirely deepest red. Nor did you dissent; you could have declined the nomination but didn't. You were the true simpleton, drawn into the communist vortex, into their subversive enterprise without realising you were being used and unaware of the risk.

"What did you do as the secretary? I remind you again that you are not obliged to say anything. But you would lose nothing by answering. You would not be revealing anything that we do not know already. It is all here in this file. I have been sitting on it, you know what I mean. You could not have done much anyway – letters to the professor in Syria and to the French newspaper. Within a week of the Salman Pak meeting, the embryonic students union was declared illegal. It was described as a communist move to foment unrest; the delegates were dispersed and Akram taken into custody charged with sedition and subversive incitement. Luckily, for him and others, there was no one from the military academy at the Salman Pak gathering, otherwise a section 89A would have been added to the charge sheet, and you know the dire consequence that would have ensued.

"I would quite believe it if you told me you knew little about what was going on behind the scenes. You were not a member of the party; the powers that be were cosying up to the National Democrats and your lot were left well alone. But there was, there is, no way of telling how long that would last. Nor can one be certain of what the ongoing investigation may throw up. New evidence may be extracted, if you know what I mean; section 89A charges may yet be added. You are a clever man, a good scholar, excelled in all your studies, but that's no substitute for the basic instinct to survive, to see the dangers ahead and reinforce one's defences, as we all have to do, and to know who your true friends are.

"Akram thought he knew but was mistaken. He had no support as he appeared before the tribunal: no lawyer to represent him, no student demonstration, no academic to plead his cause, no mention in the underground press, no bomb in a rubbish bin as he was taken to Abu Ghraib to start a five-year sentence. Abandoned by his comrades, they held themselves at a distance. The only visit he had was by a National Democrat who had acted for the illegal student union for just one week.

"I see that I have troubled you again. It's not like you to be anxious. Clear-headedness and nerves of steel, that's how I judged you the first time our paths crossed. Even then, the subversion was lurking just beneath the surface. You look puzzled. You stare at me in the face and do not recognise me. That's not altogether surprising. It was such a very long time ago, and we have so changed, I more than you. But I have not forgotten.

"How can I forget it? To you a diverting devil-daring episode, to me a life-changing event. It was the English test in the national high school examination. It was a doddle to you lot at the American School, but the inquisition and the fire to us of the Wataniyya and its useless English teachers. Some well-meaning examination administrator, probably fired with patriotic pride as he contemplated the shameful disparity between our results and yours, placed our two lots together in one room. He may have even wished inwardly that we would, how shall I put it, inspire each other! That's how it came about that you and I were seated close by, our desks almost touching. They were multiple-choice questions. In no time at all I could see that you had gone through the lot and were then sitting smugly with arms folded, while I was stuck on the first word 'neighbour', which I had never seen before. As the invigilator walked past with his back to us, I turned to you and whispered, 'What is "nigbur"?' You did not understand, so I repeated the word 'nigbur', and again you shook your head. Then something amazing happened. You leaned across, grabbed my examination paper, replaced it with yours, then got down to work. I passed the examination and obtained the certificate that in time got me where I am now instead of a lowlier job as bus inspector.

"You state in your application that you intend to study at the Sorbonne in Paris or at Nancy. It does not state whether you have been offered a place by either. Yet you were wise to apply when you did, which I see was the day after Akram attacked the warder and broke out of jail. Some may think that to be too much of a coincidence; but I do not, accepting as I do that you have always wanted to go abroad to study. There was the inevitable speculation how Akram came to have the knife and a rumour that he was helped by someone by the name of Mukhtar.

"Yes, I would give an arm and a leg to be in your position, go to France as a student. Do you think I am happy in this job? Still, it is better than being a bus inspector. If you went to France in the next few days, you would be spending several months before the start of the next academic year. But that will not be wasted time. Were I in your position, I would not delay it by a single day. I would be anxious to depart and not miss the window of opportunity to experience the delights of life in Paris as a free young man and carefree student.

"I have said much, some would say too much. You have come along with your passport. Your affairs are in order and your accounts are now settled, which must be a relief – and do I know the feeling! It is now my pleasure, with no more ado, to add the security clearance and to wish you *Bon Voyage*!"

❋ ❋ ❋

Porchester Square

After battling the arch-racists on the continent for six long years, Britain came out of the Second World War victorious, yet in the grip of austerity, shortages and rationing as well as anti-Semitism and racial prejudice. During the war there were enemy aliens kept under observation or under guard in the Isle of Man. Now there were simply aliens who came from other lands who were required to register at the Aliens Registration Office at St. James's. Resented for their apparent or presumed affluence, they were collectively called foreigners. Then, as the Festival of Britain project got under way, they were more respectfully referred to as overseas visitors.

In London's East End, Jewish population in the majority, two of the biggest national breweries were notorious for their policy of not employing Jews. A provincial barristers' chambers declined to offer a tenancy to an applicant, the head announcing the decision to his colleagues, who did not demur, "I am not having a Jew boy in my chambers." A suburban tennis club blackballed John's application for membership. When his brother, Anthony, a club member asked the reason, the secretary explained, "Your brother is Jewish!" On every working day as the courts in a major provincial city rose for lunch, judges and senior lawyers adjourned to the city's traditional gentleman's club, but not Jewish judges and lawyers who had to take lunch elsewhere.

A young man looking for digs in the 1950s scanning the many cards in street corner shop windows would find a lot of choice for about ten per cent of the world's population. For the rest there were the regrets: regret no R.C.s, regret no coloured, regret Europeans only. That very English word "regret"! How much of the sum total of good work from the

Foreign Office, the Colonial Office and the British Council was set to naught the moment a black, brown or yellow face saw the word on a card in a shop window. To an Englishman, the world beyond his shores was mostly shades of brown: darkie, coloured, half-caste, dago and wog. He would tell you proudly that the wogs started at Calais. That did not make for social cohesion. You were stuck in your ethnic group and your place on the scale of darkness. You did not want to slip down and be damned, nor aspire to climb and be rebuffed. You would then find ethnic minorities in clusters: the indigent Jew in the East End and the affluent in North London, the Chinese in the docklands, the Cypriot in Holloway, the Caribbean in Notting Hill (before the arrival of Rachman), the Irish in Kilburn, the mid-European in Bayswater, and the Middle Eastern in number 13 Porchester Square.

That was one of a terrace of mansion houses, more imposing than attractive, that backed on to Porchester Square. Number 13 may once have been the residence of a merchant or lawyer, but it was now a bed and breakfast lodging house of nine single bedrooms plus, heart of the enterprise, the basement where Mrs Bennet ruled with the help of two Irish maids. Mrs. Bennet was proud of her lodgers; she called them her paying guests. They paid the rent once a week and were served breakfast on a tray carried to one's bedroom by the maid every morning, except on the occasions when at one's request it was replaced by a meal at teatime.

There were the students, a mix of Baghdadi Jews, Iranians, Egyptians and an Afghan. And there was the odd one out, a young Welshman, who kept himself apart. He missed his valley and hated London; all that kept him was a job at the local newspaper and Donald Wolfit at the Lyric Hammersmith.

Mrs Bennet suspected that her young gentlemen were socialists or even communists. She did not approve but was prepared to be indulgent as long as they behaved; after all, it was a rite of passage for young students. Nor could politics be avoided. There was a Greek-Cypriot restaurant and a covert EOKA cell at one end of Queensway. Every Sunday you would find an elderly woman in black selling the latest edition of a locally produced newspaper, and every Sunday she would attempt to force it on you, even as you explained that you knew no Greek. At the other end of Queensway stood Porchester Hall where ballroom dancing took place on a Saturday night on the first floor, and there would often be political rallies on a Sunday in the hall proper. The hall would then fill to capacity and enthralled by the likes of Aneurin Bevan heaping disdain on those who were seeking to impose charges for spectacles and dental services – dark reactionary forces set to impair people's sight and to rot their teeth! Then as you came out onto the street, you were met by a man selling *Marxism Today* who gestured to the hall dismissively and told you prophetically, "A socialist today, a reactionary tomorrow!" As you walked back to number 13, you were met by Mrs Bennet at the street door who asked you crossly if you had been to the socialist rally. She feared they might win the next election and be returned to further ruin the country, adding that the trouble was there were just too many poor people. Yet the poor people could be counted on to be patriotic. That was demonstrated by the general fury at the Iranian "demagogue" Mosaddegh daring to steal "British" oil! The man at the barber's shop next to Royal Oak would explain to you that but for the British, the oil would have remained below the ground, undiscovered and untapped, so that "your people" would have had no benefit at all rather than what they were actually getting. He would conclude his discourse by telling you, as he tapped you lightly on the head, that "they" had no brains, no brains at all, even as you protested that you were an Iraqi, which was not quite the same.

Mrs Bennet would not have female lodgers. She saw a moral hazard in mixing the sexes as paying guests. But she had no objection to lady friends visiting, as long as they left before midnight. That was a rule often broken by the Afghan to the extent that some of his lady friends left in the early hours. As Mrs Bennet saw the situation, the young gentlemen worked hard and deserved the occasional break from their studies. They had to sow their wild oats, and it would distract them away from politics. To a lusty young man immured in a bedsitter, the only distractions were the girls, coffee-house politics, the occasional visit to the cinema and the fortnightly going to watch one's favourite football team.

In addition, there were the open spaces of Kensington Gardens and Hyde Park with its Speakers' Corner. That was a time when you believed in all innocence that one could say anything at Speakers' Corner, raise any challenge to the establishment or even be subversive with impunity. But on a Sunday evening, Speakers' Corner was essentially a spectacle. There would be the man of religion reminding you that the end was nigh. The black man telling you to free his country from colonial rule, who would invariably be told to go home by one or more. The earnest woman of the anti-vivisection league exhorting you to sign her petition. And there would invariably be a serious man with a Karl Marx beard standing on a soapbox a short distance from the rest expounding to the gathering of respectful listeners his views on world order. He would preface each sentence by, "The point is…" Then with the setting of the sun, the religious man, black man, woman and bearded man would roll, fold, pack, bundle and carry away their paraphernalia, leaving that corner of Hyde Park to darkness and the thirty-shilling women. Saleh did not approve; he thought it vulgar and risky, preferring a visit to Madame Copley's once a month after he received his money allowance. The others would tease him by asking if his loyalty might have been rewarded by a discount or Green Shield Stamps.

There was no shortage of girls and women, if you knew how to go about it. The best were the young tourists with limited time on their hands, seeking and giving pleasure with no aftermath of painful separation, guilt or embarrassment. Reuben was particularly good at it; you would often see him return to number 13 with a Swede or American in tow. David's visitor for a spell was English. He proudly confided that she was a policewoman out of uniform, and was then teased if she walked him home after a night out. But the real wonder was the Afghan. He would have a succession of long-term relationships; that is, lasting more than a week. He was not much to look at: short, thin, bespectacled, with a small straggly beard and so withdrawn that he hardly ever left his room. His assets were a nice gentle smile and the fact that he was completing his medical training at St. Mary's. Joseph, whose room was next to his, was green with envy. That was before he surrendered his virginity to Sally, a single mother, twice his age. They met at the Hammersmith Palais, did not dance, had a chat, he talking politics and she agreeing – one thing leading to another.

If there had been a Norman Tebbit then, and if he could have looked into any of the young students' hearts, the latter would at first blush have failed the test. Whenever England played against a foreign team, the young man would inwardly support the foreigners, adopt them as his team, feel a glow of vicarious pride at their runs scored and a portent of personal doom at their wickets fallen. Hardly knowing anything about the West Indies, he would gleefully hum the Calipso ditty to those "lovely pals of mine, Ramadin and Valentine" in moments of quiet reflection. But upon closer examination, the Tebbit test was itself flawed and gave rise to a misunderstanding.

The young man, favouring the opposition, did not do so out of antipathy to the English – quite the reverse. Coming from a Third World country, he was dazzled by life in London: the underground railway and moving stairs, the large buildings, the statues, the stately monuments, the public parks, the public houses, the freedom, the general good manners, and the orderly queues at bus stops and the post office. Whenever a visitor arrived from his own country, he would proudly show him around the landmarks of his London and explain the ways of his Londoners. And he adopted the ways of the host country and became progressively immersed in it to the extent that he deferred to a fellow student longer-lived in London and patronised the shorter-lived.

But, however hard he tried, there were aspects of English life that remained beyond him and he resented what he saw as the arrogance of the English, their self-assurance and their certainty of the innate superiority of their race. Sitting in the cinema waiting for a film to roll, he is brought to attention by Pathé News triumphantly showing frames of the Test match. As he hears his neighbours' exclamations of joy at a six by Dennis and of regret – "Oh, Len!" – at a dropped catch, he is reminded that he is ever an outsider.

It was otherwise the Saturday afternoon once a fortnight at Highbury. You would have put on your dirty raincoat and joined the crammed underground train to Arsenal, emerging into a packed tunnel taking you to a mass of bodies in front of the turnstiles. Then, having paid your three shillings and six pence, you stood in a mass of bodies to feast your eyes on Jimmy Logie and Cliff Holden, the rain streaming down yours and the mass of dirty raincoats without distinction. You felt at home in a strange amorphous tribe, the name itself having no obvious geographical connotation, to which you were admitted with no questions asked. It was enough that you supported the Gunners, believed with all your heart that they were superior to the Spurs, as you felt sorry for poor old Chelsea.

Saleh, who was doing a Master's, was a few years older than the rest. His was a large room on the ground floor, which often served as a common room. They would share a pot of Turkish coffee made on the gas ring and regale each other with tales of the funny ways of the English, and of the misunderstandings. Ezra spoke of arriving for a lecture in the morning when a fellow student, Anne, came to him holding boiled sweets in a crumpled paper bag, which she extended to him with a smile. "It's my birthday," she explained. Strange it was that in this country, when it was your birthday, you were a giver of gifts – not a recipient!

David spoke of his first visit to a public house with fellow students. Brian bought him a drink and insisted on paying, brushing aside David's coy reluctance to accept this act of generosity. He said, "It's our custom." But only to be followed a few minutes later by Brian pointing a finger at David and saying, "It's your turn."

Saleh spoke of his mortifying experience on his first day at college. He went with others to take lunch at a café nearby. They took their seats on the first floor. The dishes were listed on a blackboard, which Saleh read but didn't understand. He was too embarrassed to ask for advice. He was going to see what the others were ordering before making his choice. A waiter took the orders and then shouted down a dumb waiter followed by the dishes coming up. Saleh heard someone order a thing (he did not grasp what the strange word was or meant) with syrup. Two minutes later, an enticing dish of roast beef with all the trimmings and swimming in gravy emerged from the dumb waiter. When it was his turn, he told the waiter that he wanted "the something with syrup".

"Is that all you want?"

"Yes, the something with syrup."

"Do you mean (the word) with syrup?"

"Yes, just that."

The waiter bellowed "(the word) with syrup" down the dumb waiter, and within a minute or two a spotted dick with syrup was set before Saleh. He looked at it with dismay while feeling many heads turning to look at him. He started to consume the pudding nonchalantly. He was not going to incur any embarrassment by revealing his ignorance. There were worse things than missing a good lunch.

Things moved on. Some of the young men returned home. Others ended up in Canada. The Welshman fell in love with an English girl he met at the Lyric and became reconciled with life in London as he left to set up home with her.

The Afghan was the last to finish his studies and depart. The last formal event before returning home was attending the graduation ceremony at the Royal Albert Hall. He had hired a black robe from Moss Bros for the occasion and left it hanging on the hook behind the door, the sight of which impressed the maid who cleaned the room. The following morning, Eileen brought him breakfast on a tray with the addition, this time, of a red rose in a vase, which he thought touching. Then Eileen, excited and confused, asked, "Mr Abdul, are you a priest?"

He liked Eileen and did not want to disappoint her. But he wasn't going to lie. For all he knew it might be an offence to personate a priest. "Not quite," he replied.

* * *

A Question of Honour

"That was stupid. I do not understand how he could have brought himself to do it!"

Thus, the taxi driver started his monologue, which sentiment he was to maintain throughout the journey. He was referring to Zidane and the big story of the night before. It was the 2006 FIFA World Cup Final in Berlin, in which Zinedine Zidane, rated by many as the world's greatest footballer, carried the hopes of every Frenchman and the adulation and expectation of millions of fans. He scored a goal, nearly scored a second, then in the 110th minute of the game, with the scores level, he headbutted Marco Materazzi in the stomach, was shown the red card and walked off the pitch to the stadium's stunned silence.

Zidane was to explain that his reaction was in response to Materazzi first insulting his mother and then going on to impugn the honour of his sister in crude terms: "I would rather die than apologise, and I could never have lived with myself if I had let the insult be."

France went on to lose the game on penalty shoot-outs. Zidane was sentenced to a three-match suspension commuted on appeal to a three-day community service with children. He was generally forgiven by his countrymen and a proportion of them said they understood why he did it. It may not have been generally known that the brother-sister relationship holds a special place in Arab tribal culture: a woman's admiration and love of a brother are proverbial such that one would describe a passion for another as being so intense as to equal a woman's love of a brother. The brother reciprocates by being the protector of his sister's person and the guardian of her honour.

"I do not understand it," repeated the taxi driver while I recalled my meetings with Ali and Haider in 1950. It was our first year in London as students – I to study languages including English and Classical Arabic, they to be tutored in land management and water resources. I arrived by air from Baghdad, journey lasting one day. They travelled from Shatra, a tribal centre of Southern Iraq, by coach, boat and railway, their journey lasting a month. They had free time, wanted to see more of the world; and their families reposed more faith for their safety in that old mode of travel than in a BOAC's twin-propelled Argonaut. They had scratchy English between them, French not at all, so it was a devil of a job in Marseilles trying to explain in sign language that they wanted soft-boiled eggs for breakfast. When they arrived in London, they took residence in the Cumberland Hotel, only leaving some three weeks later after they discovered the self-service counters of Lyons Corner House, the way to an estate agency leading to a flat in Bayswater, and to Kardomah coffee house in Queensway.

I first saw them at Kardomah. They always kept to themselves, sitting in a corner, just as I kept to myself. None of us would take the first step. We had come from the same country, yet in some respects their Shatra was as far away from my Baghdadi suburb as Baghdad was from Paris or London. Then one day I suffered a humiliation. It was Eid, and the Kardomah put on a record of an Arabic song, the lyrics being a few words derived from an old Arab Andalusian love ode, the words sung as a refrain describing the veiled and hennaed lover.

A customer turned to me and asked the meaning.

I translated the opening words, "Behold my blood!"

Haider interjected, "Not so." Rather the true meaning was, "Avenge my blood!" He went on to recite the full couplet, "Avenge my blood! Verily, the lady of the veil. I see my blood on the tips of her fingers."

I accepted the correction as I acknowledged my mistake. The ice was broken. Thereafter, I would see them at the Kardomah from time to time, and we would occasionally on a good day go for a walk in Kensington Gardens and discuss the news from home.

Then it was the summer vacation, which they would spend at home, so it was to be a flight there and back. I told them what it felt like being carried aloft in the air, and they explained that their last preparation before joining the flight would be to receive an up-to-date report from home: what changes there had been while they were away, what new marriages, what alliances, what fallings out, what new feuds. It would not do for one to be carefree and trusting on arrival only to be gunned down without knowing what hit him and what for. Seeing my astonishment, Haider said with some bravado that a brother of his was a killer.

It was a game of backgammon in a teahouse between a cousin of Haider's and a man from another tribe, an outsider. At the same time, Haider's elder brother was sitting at another table in conversation with friends. Suddenly, an altercation arose in the middle of the game. There were accusations of cheating, voices were raised in anger, insults were exchanged, culminating in the outsider calling the cousin a pimp and impugning the virtue of his mother and sisters. At that, the cousin got up, brandished his handgun and shot the other who collapsed to the floor mortally wounded. Haider's brother, hearing the altercation and witnessing its aftermath, rushed forward from his seat with dagger raised and stabbed the prostrate dying man in the chest. Brother and cousin were arrested and charged. The case proceeded under the tribal penal code, which meant that, as with most such cases, the state authority took little interest in trial and retribution, leaving the matter to be sorted out by the families concerned and the benign involvement of the tribal elders.

Haider's father chided his killer son wanting to know why he had got involved. The son replied that he could not see his cousin involved in a fight without rallying to him. The father pointed out that the other man was fatally wounded already, was dying anyway, so what was the good of adding a stabbing? But that missed the point. It was important for the son to demonstrate publicly that he would not shrink away from standing by his cousin and sharing his cause.

It was then the turn of Ali after Haider had finished his story. But the manner of Ali's telling of the murder in his own family was quite different from Haider's. Unlike his friend's bravado, Ali recalled the painful events hesitantly, quietly and with feeling, as though the pain was still raw and felt keenly in the telling. After his father went out riding to inspect their farmland and the horse returned riderless, a search discovered him slumped in a ditch bleeding from stab wounds. He was carried home and laid in bed with the family gathered around him. A doctor was sent for, but it was hopeless; it was clear that he was on the verge of dying.

All the time, Ali's brother, the eldest of the sons, questioned the father and repeated time and again and with more and more vehemence and urgency as his life was ebbing away, "Baba, tell me who did it. You must tell me who did it. I have to know who did it." The last thing, and here Ali's voice faltered and his eyes welled, the brother in desperation gathered the loose ends of the dying man's collar, pulled his head off the pillow and called out with a raised voice, "Baba, you are dying! You must tell me before you die – else I'll kill you!"

The father shook his head, closed his eyes and breathed his last.

Then there was the traditional three days of mourning as it fell to the eldest son, now head of the family, to shoulder the burden of seeing to his deceased father's affairs, and to settle what he owed and what was owed to him. No weight rested more heavily than the need to discover the identity of the assailant or assailants so that the killing might be requited.

On the morning of the fourth day, the sister, Rim, came to the brother to tell him that she knew who had murdered their father. It was her husband and his brother. They had met the father in the field and argued over the drawing of water from the irrigation canal; tempers were frayed and knives were used. Added to the grievous loss that she shared with the family, there was also her personal torment of having to wash her husband's dishdasha besmeared with her father's blood.

By sunset of the same day, Rim had become a widow and Ahmad, her six-year-old son, an orphan. Arrests were made, charges levied, the case proceeded in the customary way of a settlement and reconciliation with barely any involvement by the state authorities. All the more so in this particular case since it was generally regarded as a family affair. And what of Rim? As part of the settlement, she was given the option and freedom to return to the bosom of her own family. She chose to remain with her in-laws because she did not want to be parted from her son.

Coming to the end of the journey, the taxi driver repeated, "That was so stupid. I do not understand how he could have brought himself to do such a thing."

I agreed. Zidane was at the pinnacle of his profession and the Berlin game was almost certainly the most important of his career. He was moved to throw that away and in the process let down his teammates, his country and his legion of adoring fans. All because of some insulting words and a reference to his mother and sister spoken in the heat of a cup-tie, and which by any sane measure meant nothing, had no effect. He should not have allowed himself to be so easily provoked; he should not have done what he did, feeling that thereby he was vindicating the family's honour. Yes, it was stupid – but, oh, the beauty of it!

* * *

The General

It so happened that I once had tea with the General here in London. That was in 1958, not long after the army coup that saw the end of the monarchy in Iraq, the massacre of king and prince regent, also Nuri al-Said, a perennial pro-British politician literally torn to pieces by a wild mob. The people behind the coup were a coalition of soft-left progressives and hard-right nationalists, represented respectively by the army officers Qasim and Arif. The well-to-do feared the former and were at first reassured in life and property by the latter. Then hot-headed Arif spoke on the radio to exalt the dawn of a new age in which there would be no rich and poor, and to declare foolishly, but no less ominously, that thenceforth expensive luxury cars would be scrapped and rich mansion houses were to be no more. That spread alarm among the landed estate owners and merchants of high worth; they rushed to consult the world atlas. Abd al-Razzaq Qadduri was one such merchant. He put his younger son on a flight to London, and that was how Thamir came to our door with our address on a piece of paper. His father's office manager was a relative of mine.

Thamir was an engaging seventeen-year-old staying at the Cumberland Hotel before enrolling at Redruth College, which the academic placement specialist had chosen for him. A choice that met his father's requirement of a quiet, gentle place of learning away from London with its large, wicked mixture of people, multitudinous attractions and easy temptations. Cornwall would be far enough away for his callow teenage son. Until then, Thamir would be seen spending several hours a day in the hotel lounge enchanted by the sight of men and women of different colours and nationalities coming and going. He now had the freedom and satisfaction as a grown, independent young man to order drinks and snacks brought to him by respectful and solicitous waiters. He would then visit me at Covent Garden where I worked and we would discuss the news of the latest happenings in Iraq.

On a few evenings, he came to have dinner with us. I had been married for a year and living in Ham Common. It was a long distance away, but that didn't put off Thamir. It meant experiencing the wonder of the underground, the top deck of the London red bus and seeing more of London and Londoners. On his second visit, he brought my wife a brooch that he had bought in the hotel.

She was delighted and half-protested, "You shouldn't have! What is it for?"

He may have meant to say that it was for our hospitality and friendship; it came out as, "It's because you are beautiful," and she glowed.

Then, Tariq, Thamir's elder brother, also arrived in London with some others. They were staying at The Churchill. I went with Thamir to spend the afternoon with them. I found that the others were Tariq's father-in-law, Nurredin Mahmud, and his son called Zaid. This Nurredin was the General, former Prime Minister, butcher of the 1952 popular uprising.

There have been several uprisings since the foundation of the pro-British monarchy in 1932, witnessed in succession by the eternal Tigris. There would be an uprising at one of its banks and the news would reach the disaffected on the other. They would rise to join the uprising but be prevented by riot police blocking the bridge. There would be a standoff, then an uncontrollable surge, and shots would be fired and blood spilt. The government would fall to be replaced by another who would offer temporary concessions leading to the insurgents returning to their offices, schools, shops and market stalls. And the Tigris that had seen it all would continue to flow while waiting for the next one.

The 1952 uprising had been particularly violent. It came very close to being a revolution. Starting as a peaceful demonstration calling for reforms at home and neutrality in foreign affairs, it was soon taken over by the communists whipping up popular discontent and confronting the lines of riot police with the cry, "We want bread, not bullets!"

On November 23, the insurgents stormed and destroyed two police stations, and then moved to the city's main thoroughfare and sacked the US Information Centre. Their next intended target being the British Embassy across the river, they came up against a mass of riot police at the road leading to the bridge. This caused panic in the palace and the powers behind it. There was a swift reaction: the cabinet was dismissed, the army was called in and General Nurredin Mahmud was given the mandate to form a new government. That was an inspired choice given what was to follow.

The General was a Kurd by descent and a Turk by type, had no association with any of the political parties, nor was he identified with any of the faiths, sects, tribes and subtribes of which Baghdad was constituted. He forthwith proclaimed martial law, dissolved all political parties, locked up their leaders and ordered arrests all over Baghdad. There was a mass demonstration the day after with banners proclaiming "Down with the dictatorship of the English spy Nurredin Mahmud". The General's response was uncompromising and brutal. At his personal order, the troops opened fire on the crowds, killing eighteen and wounding eighty in one day in the plebeian quarter of Bab al-Sheikh. At the same time, military tribunals were set up to dispense summary judgement throughout Iraq. By the end of the week, according to an official count, there were 958 thrown into jail, 2041 in detention awaiting their turn and 2 condemned to death. That put an end to the insurrection, and in January 1953, barely two months after his appointment, the General stepped down from the premiership and returned to the barracks.

The General was a good host. After the introductions he offered me a cigarette, commented on the weather, asked me how long it had been since I was last in Iraq and what I thought of life in England. That gave me the opportunity to ask how long they would be staying in London. He said he wasn't sure, that he had an appointment for a consultation in Harley Street. Zaid, who was less restrained, interjected to indicate what his father was too guarded to divulge, that their stay depended on what was happening back home. Thamir told them that my wife worked at the BBC, and Tariq asked me what I thought of Qasim and on whose side he was. By way of further clarification, he asked me if I knew for which world power Qasim was acting. I said I did not know and queried the question by asking, "Why should one assume that every Iraqi politician or leader was an agent of a foreign power?" I turned to the General and asked him if he agreed; he nodded. He then added that Qasim would be committing a serious mistake if he put his trust in any foreign power. They will use him, then cast him aside once they had no more use for him. Tariq said they would chew him up, then spit him out. The General was displeased by the metaphor, it showed on his face, and said he wouldn't put it quite like that.

It was now Thamir's turn. When asked about his studies, he mentioned that he would be going to Cornwall but was happy to stay at the Cumberland in the meantime and enjoy the experience of walking the streets of London and getting to know life in England. Tariq said it must be a relief after the incident that his younger brother had witnessed and which hastened his departure. Thamir now related what happened.

He had heard a commotion in Taher Street not far from where they lived. He was drawn towards it and found a large, unruly mob shouting outside the house of Kamil al-Chaderchi. They were his supporters celebrating the army coup and in particular the death of his and their mortal enemy, the "British agent and spy" Nuri al-Said. Some were waving Nuri's body parts exultantly. Al-Chaderchi came out onto the balcony to address them. He praised them for their loyalty and political resolve but pointed out gently that to desecrate the dead, whomever he might be, was a *haram*. Feeling the rebuke, some shouted back that they had suffered so much under the rule of the tyrant, and the succession of other corrupt and brutal leaders who had sold out to foreign enemies, that they could not be expected to show restraint. This was coupled with the cry, "Down to Imperialism; death to English spies!"

As Thamir finished speaking, the General said that he believed al-Chaderchi to be a decent man even though he had not met him, that he had no ill feeling towards him as a person, but he had to have him locked up in the 1952 insurrection because he could make no distinction between him and the other party leaders. I did not let on that until I left Iraq, two years before this insurrection, I had been a member of al-Chaderchi's National Democratic Party.

I asked Zaid what he thought of the little he had seen of London. He said that England seemed strange to him even though he was born in London. This gave him the right to claim British citizenship, but he would not do so. Before the General could stop him, he blurted out that the family had had a long spell in London while his father held the position of military attaché at the embassy. The General closed that line of conversation by saying that it had been a long time since and he could barely remember it. He said (I thought rather too vehemently) that he'd had no contact with any of his old English acquaintances who may not know of his arrival in England.

Changing the subject, the General asked me where in Baghdad was our home and who were our neighbours, which I understood referred to our particular *mahalla* or quarter. Under the surface, Baghdad consisted of different self-administered quarters, each having its own mukhtar who was supposed to know and could testify to the character of every member of the *mahalla*. Each *mahalla* had its own leading family, its particular sect or ethnic grouping, and some *mahallat* had their own historical mosque as a focal point. In answering that question, I could not resist the temptation to add that our *mahalla* was not very far from Bab al-Sheikh and asked the General if he was familiar with it. This was received in utter silence while I thought of the men whom I knew, left-wing activists including communists, some my friends, who had operated there. The silence was broken after a while by the General getting out his cigarette case and extending it to me, which I declined. He lit one for himself, drew a long pull, reclined back and expounded that Baghdad had grown so over the years that there were now more *mahallat* than mosques, unlike the situation in smaller towns such as his own, Sulaymaniyya. Again, I couldn't avoid the temptation to add a little mischief. I said that in our modern times the focal point of any *mahalla*, and any grievance, was the police station. They all agreed. After a short pause, the General said that in his book anyone who attacked a police station was guilty of treason and deserved no mercy. He said it was otherwise with people demonstrating peacefully and not being subversive. That led to a further mention of Kamil al-Chaderchi, his party appeared to be the principal beneficiary of the latest army coup, a big change from 1952 and his then detention as a party leader. The General said that he did not have it in mind at the time to keep the opposition leaders in detention for longer than was necessary. He intended to set them free just as soon as things had calmed down. In retrospect, he regretted that he did not remain Prime Minister long enough to make a difference. Hearing that, the chance was too good to miss, so I asked him what he thought was his greatest achievement as Prime Minister. He replied, with a show of modesty, that he could not think of any real achievement for which he would claim credit.

He was corrected by Zaid who said, "Baba, have you forgotten that you brought down the price of tomatoes?"

The General responded to that animatedly. He explained that he always did the shopping at his local greengrocers. One morning, he went over to buy a pound of tomatoes and found that the price was almost twice what he was charged the week before. They couldn't explain the reason for the increase, so he concluded that some profiteering was afoot – people taking advantage of the political unrest. Later that day, in his capacity of Prime Minister, he issued an edict halving the price of tomatoes. I asked him if it held and for how long. He said it did hold at his local greengrocer's throughout his premiership. I asked him if he could not have done the same for bread, given the agitation surrounding it. He said he judged that there was no shortage of bread at reasonable prices. He observed that bread was used as justification during every insurgency throughout the course of human history, which was false in nearly every case. It reached the stage that whenever he heard a crowd of people shouting "Give us bread", he felt it was time to reach for his gun. I resisted the temptation to bring up the historical allusion "Let them eat cake!"

The discussion was concluded by the General's authoritative statement regarding bread and tomatoes. There was nothing more to say. The General got up and we rose with him. He led us to the dining room where English high tea was waiting.

❊ ❊ ❊

Christmas

It was a carvery buffet dinner. I carried a heaped plate shamefacedly to the nearest alcove and occupied the very end of the leather-upholstered bench that extended the length of one side. Halfway through the mound of vegetables, I paused to take stock of the situation. There were two tables across the other side with eleven people whom I judged to be together but not one party. They were of varying ages, perhaps neighbours meeting for a drink on a Friday evening at their local. It was fairly early and they were generally sedate. The exception was the woman immediately in front of me, her back towards me, talking animatedly between taking sips of Coca-Cola. There were occasional breaks in her exposition. Those were the times when the young man (in comparison, a boy) across the table from her would have the chance to expound on some serious matter with assumed gravity and confidence. The others were silent throughout. The seat in the corner, furthest away from the woman, was occupied by the only other female, perhaps in her early twenties, who appeared not to be listening. There were occasions when I thought I caught surreptitious looks of her disapproval in the woman's direction.

At the next table, they were talking quietly as they addressed their pints with gusto. All apart from the wrestler who was taking his time between small, delicate sips. I thought of him as a wrestler because of his rotund figure, bald bullet head and the podgy hand cradling his pint glass. He sat at the end, level with the woman, the pair separated by the two feet between their tables.

The woman was besotted with the wrestler. After making a statement, she would turn around and repeat it to him. From time to time, she would lean over to dig him in the ribs.

If he ignored her, which he mostly did, she would beat his muscular torso with her fists to gain his attention. On one occasion she got up, stood behind him, put her arms around his neck and leaned over to whisper in his ear. He then got up and walked out of the alcove. She resumed her seat at the table with her back towards me. The wrestler returned with a glass of Coca-Cola, which he set before her.

A little later, she pushed her chair closer to his. Placing her arm on the armrest, it touched the wrestler's arm positioned on his. She leaned further and took hold of his hand; he held her hand for a few seconds and smiled at her. The wrestler's attitude was one of impassivity. I got the impression he was more embarrassed than annoyed by the woman's attention and provocation. That was particularly evident when she let go of his hand and rested hers high up on his thigh, again evoking no response. I noticed that there were no rings on her fingers.

By and by, the woman's talk subsided leaving the field clear for the boy. Her agitation now took the form of springing up from her chair (in doing so, revealing to me a thick band of white flesh between her jeans and top), hopping across to touch or say something to the wrestler before resuming her seat.

Until then I had only seen her back. I had the impression that she was past her prime, that she may have given up as she put on the years and unintended layers of flesh along with them. I was particularly struck by the sight of her brassiere, whose straps I could discern through the thin blouse digging deep into her flanks.

Eventually, the drink was having its effect on the others. Each one was now confronting his or her own demons. No one was in the mood to listen; the woman was distressed. She seemed to look but no longer connect with the others. She leapt out of her chair, moved across, but received no reaction from the wrestler. Her glances desperately darted everywhere. She suddenly saw me for the first time in the corner behind her. She glanced at me, saw a solitary old man, looked away but then immediately looked back again with a swift reassessment. She lurched towards me.

"Are you happy?" she asked.

"Yes."

"Really, really happy?"

"Yes. I am happy."

"I am happy for you." She sat next to me and resumed. "Are you enjoying yourself?"

"Yes. I am enjoying myself."

"That's nice."

"Do you come here often?"

"Only occasionally."

"Do you live around here?"

"I live in Roundhay." I had to repeat that.

The woman turned her head towards the others. "He lives in Roundhay."

I asked her where she lived.

She said, "We live around here, in the Red Hall's." She asked me to guess how old she was but stopped me before I replied by adding, "I want to know what you really, really, honestly think."

I said, "Mid-thirties."

She said, "Forty-five, I am forty-five."

I said that forty-five was still young. She did not agree, so I tried to reassure her. I said that forty-five was young, looking at the matter from the height in which I was. That was an opening; she could have asked me how old I was, but she didn't. Throughout our conversation I was struck by her reticence, a delicacy and caution, as regards certain matters. But there was none of that as she kept on expressing unhappiness with the weight of years that she was carrying.

She suddenly changed the subject. "I have no children," she said. "We tried, but couldn't have any."

When she said "we" she pointed to the wrestler. I asked if he was her man. She said yes, but they weren't married. I said it must be a long relationship. She said yes, they had been together for ten years. I said I could tell that she was very much in love with him. She said she loved him madly, and added rapidly that he also loved her. She repeated that they could not have children. I asked if they had tried any of the medical procedures that were available, and again I was impressed by her cautious reply. "It wouldn't have been any good." She said she had to accept that. I said that she was lucky to have the love and protection of a good man. She said yes, he loved her, then added that Craig (that was his name) was seven years younger than her. I said that did not matter. She laughed and added, "He is my toy boy." She said her name was Pauline. She did not ask to know my name.

She changed the subject again and asked me how I was spending Christmas. I said I would be having it with my daughter. She asked if my daughter would visit us, and I explained that I was now on my own and would be going to my daughter's house. She said that was nice. Again, I was impressed by her delicacy as she said it was a good thing to spend it with one's family and not be all on one's own. I said it had been almost three years, and she said she was sorry.

She then asked, "Do you miss her?"

"Yes, I miss her," I replied.

She said they would be going to some of Craig's relatives on Christmas day and implied it might not go well without expanding any further. She changed the subject again and pointed to the boy. "He is gorgeous. Don't you think he is gorgeous?"

"Yes, he is good-looking."

"He is gorgeous, but you are handsome."

I said that at my age it wasn't something I cared about.

But she insisted, "He is gorgeous, but you are handsome."

"Perhaps it could have been said that I was handsome when I was young," I replied.

She said, "You are handsome. I bet you were a killer when you were young." She repeated that the boy was gorgeous and added, "I don't know what's the matter with him," but went no further.

In the meantime, Craig, having left the alcove, had now returned and came to stand in front of us, I thought in a somewhat challenging manner.

I hastened to say, "Hello, Craig, she has been telling me how much she loved you." I extended my hand, which he shook after a moment's hesitation. He turned around without saying a word and sat nearby in the seat that Pauline had vacated. I suggested that Pauline ask Craig to join us. She did, but he declined. He seemed to me to be confused and overwhelmed by my sudden intrusion, a strange man, in his domestic life. I suggested to Pauline that Craig was the strong, silent type of man. She liked that and repeated, so he could hear it, "A strong, silent man."

She reverted back to her age. She said she'd had a lot of fun when she was young. I said forty-five was still young, and there was a whole life of fun and happiness before her.

She pleaded, "Do you think so?"

For the first time, I turned to look at her full in the face. Between the clumps of golden hair falling haphazardly down to her shoulders, I saw a gentle attractive face, the face of the young and beautiful girl and woman she once was.

"You are beautiful," I said.

"I am old."

"No you are not. You are beautiful."

"But he is gorgeous," she said pointing to the boy, "and you are handsome."

"You are attractive."

"Do you really think so?"

"Yes."

"I am forty-five."

"You have such an attractive face."

She brushed the strands of hair away from her face. "You should have seen me when I was young."

"I see you now as you were then."

"That's lovely." Seeing me look at my wristwatch, she said, "Do you have to go?"

"Yes."

"You're not driving, are you?"

"Yes, I shall be driving."

"But you mustn't drive."

"I've only had a half of cider."

"That's all right, then."

As I got up, she got up with me. I realised with a start that all other conversations had stopped. There was a general stillness and most eyes were averted. I crossed over, that is took the two steps, to where Craig was sitting with his eyes downcast. I put my hand on the back of his chair and said, "If I had been thirty years younger, I would have been a competitor." Everyone laughed. Craig lifted his head and smiled, the smile of a proud, strong, silent man. Pauline took hold of my hand, pulled me towards her and planted a kiss on my cheek. I wished everyone a merry Christmas and heard the responses as I walked away.

❊ ❊ ❊

I Am So Lucky

"What a marvellous view," said the man as he sat on one of the benches overlooking the full vista of Filey Bay.

"You can't beat it," said the woman sitting close by, walking frame propped up against the next bench. She took his observation to be a welcome invitation to a chat; an opportunity to relate her life story. "You can't beat it, but I wish the wind wasn't so cold. I shall not want to go back to West Yorkshire. I used to come here nearly every day. Now I don't go out much, mostly one day a week, the Thursday, after the post office. There's usually a queue. When it's my turn, they smile and ask how I am and talk about the weather. You can't stop long though because of the people behind waiting their turn.

"This morning, the woman in front of me was paying for her telly. She turned, looked at me and said, 'You are lucky, you don't have to pay.' The cheek of it! I would then cross over and get the bread from Coupland, then a little meat from Overtons next door. I tell them to add a pork pie. They do such good pies. I get the smallest, the sixty pence one, which Elsie lets me have for fifty.

"Yes, it's a lovely view but I wish it were less windy. Still, it must be good for those sailing boats you see over there. I don't know what the fishermen make of it as they take their cobles very early out to sea. Look, look at the seagulls, they are so cheeky. Some will even swoop down to pinch the food out of your hands. They're encouraged by the people who bring their fish and chips to sit and eat them here out of their wrappers.

"No, you won't see me go back to West Yorkshire. It's seventeen years since we left Bradford, Arthur and me. Not

Bradford exactly, more the country. Except it wasn't what you would call the country. Just some fields, which they then covered in houses and gave to just anybody. My daughter said she wouldn't want her son to go to the local school. She said she would so love him to go private. I said, 'Don't be daft, where will you get the money?' She said they did the pools every week.

"She then said there was this house in West Avenue over there with four bedrooms. I said I bet they'd want eighty. So she asked and they told her just that, eighty thousand pounds. Of course they didn't have the money, so she said we could sell our house and they would sell theirs. She said I would have the ground floor and they'd have the rest. Of course I'd need to have the ground floor, what with the hip and heart murmur. Mr Gupta said he'd done a good job; the new hip will be good for at least ten years. He said it might have to be redone later. I had to wait to have it done, but not as long as some others had to.

"Arthur didn't want us to sell. 'I'm not moving,' he said. We told him he'd like Filey and the sea air would be good for his asthma. 'And what about my allotment?' he asked. I said, 'What allotment?' He had given it up at the end of the previous summer, what with his knees and his asthma, and they had put it up to fifteen. He then said he'd miss his mates and Park Avenue on a Sunday when there was a game of cricket. That was before they stopped playing cricket altogether at Park Avenue. Our daughter asked him if he wouldn't miss his family, especially his new grandson, if they went and we stayed behind. I reminded him that we were getting on – and what with my hip and heart, I might die before him, then who would be there to look after him. So he agreed. He said he would do it for the family. And he said he remembered once going to the Scarborough annual cricket festival, which he enjoyed.

"So we agreed to buy the house for the asking price, which we would have once we'd sold our houses. We put the houses on the market, and eventually we sold ours and moved to our daughter's. It had been agreed beforehand that whoever sold first, they would move in with the others until the others had also sold theirs. But it took them such a long time waiting for a buyer. The people who were selling us the house then took it off the market. They said they had waited three years and weren't going to wait any more. At least that's what our daughter told us. She said she asked, and that's what she was told. So with the money we got for our house, we bought a bungalow here in the Wharfedales, you know, near where the school is. They're now building so many more houses nearby. I don't right know where they'll get the people to fill all of them.

"My daughter then told us they weren't moving. They had changed their minds. They would remain in West Yorkshire. They took their house off the market. I loved the bungalow but couldn't stop there after Arthur passed away. And my hip, the one that Mr Gupta had done, was playing up. I sold and went to live in a flat on the ground floor off Mitford Street. That was near the shops, but I wasn't happy. The bathroom was right at the back, almost in the yard, and I had other problems, not just the hip, which had to be redone.

"I took the bus to Scarborough to see a Dr Martin. I had to go more than once. It is so good to have the bus pass, and the money they give you in winter for the heating – it makes such a difference. Dr Martin said it would be difficult to redo the hip. He said there was no guarantee that it would be all right. So I said, 'Dr Martin, are you telling me that I will be in a wheelchair the rest of my life?' He said he'd see what could be done. I was lucky. He put in a metal something or other, so I have no pain, not much anyway, but now I have to walk with this frame. I also have cancer.

"I was then given one of the flats in Chapel Court. There are only three of us left now. I didn't want the one next to the street, so they let me have the one to the side with a little patch of garden. I'd wheel myself there on a good day and sit on the bench. People passing in the street can see me. They wave to me sometimes. The warden comes around once a week. He asks me if I need anything from the shops. The home help comes in the afternoon. She isn't the same woman every time. The people from Boots get the prescription and bring the pills to my door. The people here are so kind; they don't hurry you as you try to cross the road. I love my flat. Why would I want to go back to West Yorkshire? I am so lucky."

❄ ❄ ❄

Downsizing

As he packed the car and checked the fuel gauge, the sun came out from behind the clouds. Feeling it as one of his better days, he decided to walk across to his favourite clifftop terrace at the end of Queen Street in the old part of town for a final view of the scenery, there to rest awhile before walking back and the drive home.

It is a narrow terrace with a line of adjacent benches overlooking the full vista of the bay. His favourite bench was unoccupied. In fact, the only other person he could see was a woman, whom he judged to be middle-aged, sitting at another bench further into the terrace engrossed in a book.

Just as he was about to get up to retrace his steps, the woman came up to him and handed him the book saying, "I've finished with it, would you like to have it?"

It was a small booklet, the sort you get from the town's information centre, with the title *Filey Bay Today* and the price of fifty pence on the cover.

"I'll pay you for it," he said.

She brushed that aside with a smile, turned and started walking away towards the other end of the terrace. She then stopped, hesitated, came back and asked if he would help her with some directions. He nodded, and she sat at the next bench, close to him, with the armrests between them. She enquired for the way to the medieval St. Oswald's Church, wondered if it would be open and if it was worth a visit. She explained that she had come to that part of Filey to look at an old house nearby which she understood was on the market, only to discover that it had been sold.

"It could have been what I'm looking for," she said, getting into her stride, "with a small yard at the back for a dog. I could just about manage the asking price of eighty thousand. I can perhaps retire on a small pension in four years' time, but as they've put up the pension age to sixty-seven, I would then have to wait seven more years before receiving the state one. In the meantime, I have to find a place of my own. I'm now living in Hunmanby. It's my parents' house; they say they want to downsize.

"It's four years since I went back to Hunmanby. That was after I finished with Bill. No, I can't say I am divorced; we never were married, but we lived together for nineteen years. I don't know how I managed to put up with it all that time. We both work for the army as civilians, I as a clerical assistant, Bill as a mechanic. That was how we met. Our first home was in Beverley, which was convenient for the barracks. No, it wasn't the smart Beverley that you know, with the Minster, cobbled streets and big houses. Ours was a grim, poor, shabby end of town, and it was hellish. Neighbours from hell? Yes, we had them as well, and I suffer from bad nerves. We then moved to a nice bungalow on an estate in Driffield. Bill loved it, but that was when the real trouble started. What with looking after it and the mortgage, we were always in debt. I had to deal with letters from the bank, find the money at the end of every quarter for the gas and electricity, juggle the credit cards, and we always fell behind with the monthly council tax payments.

"I kept on suggesting that we downsized, but he wouldn't have it. He said he loved the bungalow and wouldn't want to give it up ever. I kept on saying that we'd never be free of debt problems until we stopped using the credit cards. He would agree, start to cut down and reduce the balance, but would then see that there was some unutilised credit and do another splurge. I did everything: cleaning, decorating, washing and ironing, and, after returning from work in the evening, I had to do the cooking, clear the table with the washing up to follow. He wouldn't lift a finger to help. I even had to clean his car, as well as do the gardening; he would only mow the grass.

"As the years rolled by, I became more and more anxious to have a child. We couldn't have it at the beginning, we were that poor. Later, I suggested we would downsize, I would retire and we could then start a family. But Bill wouldn't agree. He wasn't going to sell the bungalow; besides, he didn't like children. We got a dog at Christmas, which meant more work. I had to get up very early in the morning to feed it, walk it, and then go back to make the breakfast, clear the table before getting in the car with Bill to start another day at work.

"I never saw much of Bill, neither at the weekends or on work-free days. I don't think he was unfaithful. His passion was his car, also his motorbike. He is a very good mechanic; there is nothing he doesn't know about cars. His mates often ask him to look at their cars and motors when anything goes wrong. As I wanted to improve the situation, I got us to join the National Trust so we could get in the car at least once a month to visit one of the big country houses. I said I would make the sandwiches and other snacks, have coffee in a thermos, put the lot in a basket together with a tablecloth and napkins. We could then drive as far as Derbyshire and return all in one day. We did that once, which I enjoyed, but he was on the phone to his mates all the time. He didn't want to do it again.

"You may well ask if I loved him. How can I answer that question? Was I really in love, or was I just afraid of losing him? Every day of those nineteen years, I woke up in the morning and went to bed at night with the dread that he would tire of me, would leave me so that I would be on my own. Yet it was more than that. I cared for him, wanted him to be happy. Much as I felt unhappy about the work, the exhaustion, the hardship, the money problems and the anxieties affecting my nerves, and as much as I complained about the lack of appreciation and neglect, I realised in the last four years that I was getting my emotional reward from those very things I did unstintingly for Bill – to protect him, help him and please him. He was the child I never had.

"That didn't stop me from making a big mistake and confessing it to Bill. I said it was that I felt neglected and unloved. I said it won't happen again, but I wanted us to downsize, live more to a budget, so I could retire and have more time to cope with things. I said I would leave him if he didn't allow me to do that. I dreaded his reaction to my admission.

"What a fool I was. How little did I understand? It was even worse, more cruel, than I had feared. He was just indifferent. He said he'd had enough of my nagging and my nerves, unlike the wife of Steve, his best friend, who was a Thai and never complained. I told him if that was how he felt, then he should ask Steve to get *him* a Thai woman. And you know what his reply was? Can you believe it? He said I should speak to Steve's wife myself. That hurt even if he didn't really mean it.

"That was the end of our lives together. We put the bungalow on the market and found willing buyers. Just before the contracts were exchanged, Bill stupidly told them that we were desperate to sell and not to wait – so they forced us to reduce the price from two hundred thousand to one hundred and sixty. That reduced my share, after paying off the mortgage, by twenty thousand. I asked Bill to keep the dog, but he refused. He said it was my dog, so I had to care for it. My parents said they didn't want it because my father is allergic to dogs. So I had to get rid of it.

"You ask me again if I loved Bill. Yes, I did and was very unhappy when we separated; and even more so when I learnt that he'd got himself a Filipina. I bump into him at work from time to time. That's another reason why I think of taking early retirement. They already have one child and another on the way. So that's a double whammy for me! But with the passage of time, the hurt has become less, and so has the love that I had for him. But I still care for him; I can't help it. I've had several relationships since then. They were a disappointment. They tell you they're single, then you discover that they're married, or in a relationship, or not interested long-term, just using me.

"My parents keep talking about downsizing. My father says he will soon be seventy and doesn't want them to stay where they are.

"I do miss not having a companion. There's Victoria who I met at the social club. We go out shopping in Scarborough and to the theatre. We like Alan Ayckbourn. We've got to the stage that we're so used to his style that we can anticipate a new turn in the play just before it happens; we dig each other to signal it, as happened when we were watching a production of *A Chorus of Disapproval* at the Stephen Joseph Theatre last month. I'm glad you also like Ayckbourn. There's a performance of his *Snake in the Grass* here in Filey tonight at the Evron Centre."

The man now looked at his wristwatch and said it was time for him to drive back to Leeds and that his car was parked at a metered bay. They got up and walked slowly to Queen Street.

She said, "I've not made up my mind who to vote for in the election. There's a hustings in Hunmanby tomorrow. That will be exciting. I shall have one or two questions to ask. Which reminds me, I haven't asked you if you're single. I guess my father will be there, too; he will ask about housing, which is his pet subject. To tell you the truth, I think they want to downsize because of me. When they took me in after I separated from Bill, they couldn't have imagined I would still be living with them four years later."

They stopped by her car parked in Queen Street. She thanked him for listening patiently to her tale of woe. She then asked, "When will you be back in Filey? No, don't tell me. I shall come to Filey next Thursday. I have an appointment at the hairdresser's at ten and will be meeting Victoria at twelve; we've arranged to visit Sledmere House. If I should come to the terrace at all for the view, it will be between eleven and twelve."

He wished her well. She told him to take care as he walked away.

* * *

A Hard Man

I have been running this business for six weeks. I want to set up a steak bar one day, after I've saved enough. The landlord lets me use the kitchen to prepare the lunches. I pay him a little rent, and the arrangement suits us both. The customers who drop in for a drink see my menu, can order their lunch and then wait at the bar for me to make it for them. I already have a few regulars.

I am known as Joe. I hate the name Joseph, but it's too late to change it. It's already in so many written records. My father's name is Eugene; there is a Saint Eugene's Cathedral in Derry. My mother is from Shipley and our home was in Bradford. There were four of us children: a girl, a boy, then me followed by my younger sister. I am the black sheep of the family. The trouble I caused them! I don't blame my parents. We were poor, but they looked after us and provided: our father in the building trade and our mother a cleaner.

They did what they could to correct me, chastise me, like all parents do to discipline their kids. I got more beatings from Mother than Father. But what can you expect living in Holmewood. You must have heard of the Holmewood and Brierley Estates. They were in the papers almost every day. I didn't belong to any gang, I wasn't old enough for that.

When I was ten, I burnt another lad and was sent to borstal. There was a little waste ground behind the garage and some overturned empty kerosene drums, except that there was a little left at the bottom in some of them. After he stepped into one, I struck a match. He was badly burnt at the front and in the face. That will last him a lifetime. I didn't feel bad about it, nor sorry for him. He said something to annoy me. It was his fault, as I saw it. My father told the court that they did all they could to put a stop to my mischief and the lawyer said it was a tragic accident – but I knew better.

I am now fifty and have been to court more times than I can remember. I committed all the offences against a person that you would find in the book: assault, actual bodily harm, GBH, wounding. I never felt remorse about any of them. I've had regrets, but not remorse. I did what I did because of what they did to me. I wouldn't start it myself – but if anyone hurt me, then I couldn't rest until I paid them back. You know what pebble-dash is? There was one who hurt me, so I pushed him against the wall and scraped his face. He had to have plastic surgery. I don't feel anything about these things. Nor would I feel sentimental if someone did me a good turn; most of the time, I'm not aware that they are good turns.

A thing is done, and once done that's the end of it. I don't have troubled sleep thinking about it. I stopped going to church as soon as I changed into long trousers. Yes, I have a bad temper, the social report in court called it "explosive". I got it from Mother. I can be provoked by a single word, even if not addressed to me. Once I was sitting in the pub with a drink in front of me. A man came along, pointed to another and called him a thieving bastard in a loud voice. I got up and told him to mind his language, then I said another word and I'll thump him. He apologised saying that he didn't mean it and he hadn't addressed it to me anyway. I said I don't want to hear those two words again. I've never committed a property offence. I have nothing but contempt for those who steal, burgle or cheat. I've only ever taken cars, for which I appeared in court many times, but that's different.

I spent six years in borstal. I hated it. Hard though it was on the outside, it was even rougher on the inside. They were mostly petty thieves, and I would get into scrapes with them. It was very hard at the beginning, but it got a little better as you learnt how to control your temper and work the system. No one from my family came to see how I was getting on. Towards the end I would get points for good conduct, which I accumulated. When there was enough, they allowed me to go home on a visit. By then my parents had been evicted by the council, so they came to start a new life in Filey.

You know what, I cannot remember what my first job was when I came out of borstal. I did many odd jobs while on benefits. Then I got a job at the Thistle Hotel. That was the best job I ever had. They put me in the kitchens, and I found that I was good at it and enjoyed it. I stayed with them for six years and learnt a lot about food and catering. I created my own dishes, which were appreciated.

Then there was a burglary. Someone broke into the office and stole the takings. They set up an investigation and there were interviews. The police were called; they checked my criminal record. The manager asked me what I knew about the robbery, where precisely I was that night and what I was doing. He then asked me point-blank if I had taken any of the money. I got up, lunged at him across the desk and fisted him in the face. He screamed and shouted for help. I turned away and walked out for good.

I went back to live on the dole in-between odd jobs, but mostly I did the "doors". There were so many clubs operating in the summer in Scarborough. My two sons now do the doors. The P, S, C and B tattoos you see on my arm stand for Phyllis, Stan, Charles and Bernadette. They're over twenty, yet they still call me from time to time asking, "Dad, can you give me some money?" But I haven't heard from Phyllis after she went down to London. I want this business to succeed so I can make money for the grandchildren. I expect there will be some by the time I've saved enough, set up the steak bar and got it going.

I am now happily divorced. It was a disaster. I mostly blame her relatives. They turned her against me, told her she could have done better. Whatever I gave her, she said it wasn't enough. So I had to go away to look for a better-paid job. When I got back, there wasn't much of a welcome. I had no idea what she was up to while I was away. That happened once, then twice. When it was the same thing the next time, I went upstairs and put my things in a suitcase. She asked what the case was for. I told her I couldn't take any more and left for good. I divorced her and they gave her custody of the children. For ten years she wouldn't let me see them. Then the social people intervened; they were going to take them into care because she was always on the bottle. Instead, the custody was transferred to me.

The marriage left me bitter. I can have brief, occasional affairs but nothing enduring. I cannot trust any woman enough for me to make a commitment. They, in turn, say I'm a hard man. But I'm not really. I'm my own man and keep my feelings to myself; I'm happy to be left alone. I only want to hit back if I'm hurt. I'm not entirely without feelings for others.

Once I saw a woman have money snatched from her hand as she turned away from the cashpoint. I chased the thief and caught him. I gave him a good hiding. He said I was hurting him. I called him a thieving bastard who deserved it. I then let go of him and returned the money to her. The other day, I saw a woman slumped in the middle of the road in Scarborough. She wasn't well, so I picked her up in my arms, carried her to a bench and stayed with her until the ambulance arrived.

I've kept out of trouble for the last two years. I came to live in Filey to be near my parents. I have my own rented flat. Every day, when I finish here at six, I go to see how they are. I help with all the work in their bungalow: decorating, putting up new shelves, sweeping and changing the light bulbs. They are frail, Mother more than Father. She is seventy-six and he is eighty-one, but she's the one who wears the trousers.

She tells me how much she loves me and calls me her good boy. But she still has her bad temper, the one I inherited from her. It's not as fiery as when I was young. Like when I was ten and she asked me to get the money from Auntie. She had lent her some and now wanted it back, so she sent me. But Auntie didn't give me the money. She said she would be seeing Mother and would give it to her then. On the way back I found a fiver in the street, so I went to the corner shop and loaded up with sweets and pop. As soon as I got home with the carrier bags, Mother asked me where the money was. I told her she didn't give it to me. She slapped me and called me a liar and a thieving bastard. She walloped me all the way up the stairs, then at the top of the stairs, and down the stairs, all the way to the street door. That evening she and Father went to the pub and met Auntie. They brought me back a big bag of crisps and an enormous bottle of pop. I couldn't eat the crisps because my lips were cut and my face was puffed up, nor could I drink because my throat hurt. So my brother and sisters had the lot. The next day, when no one was looking, I shoved my young sister out of the window. That was on the first floor. Then I found a box of matches lying about. I put it in my pocket and made my way to the spare ground behind the garage looking for mischief.

* * *

Leonarda

There were two tables, each with a pair of chairs, set touching each other on the pavement of a seaside restaurant. I occupied one of the tables, all alone. Next to me, almost touching, sat a man and his female companion across the table from him.

Seeing the headline in the folded *Le Figaro* on my table, with the word "LEONARDA" writ large, the man became agitated and pointed an accusing finger at the paper. "That's not right."

The incident was on nearly everyone's lip that day. A girl of fifteen had spent five years in France with her illegal immigrant Roma family. Then, after they had exhausted the legal asylum process, they were apprehended and deported to Kosovo. In the case of Leonarda, the arrest by the police took place as she travelled on a bus taking her and fellow students on a school outing.

"It's not right," repeated the man.

"Yes, a bit rough," I said.

"It is incorrect," he rejoined. "I don't know why they keep on referring to her as a Kosovar."

"You mean she is a Roma?"

"That, certainly. Besides, she had no connection at all with Kosovo."

"Do I take it you are a Kosovar? I compliment you on your good French."

"Yes, I am, arrived years ago. All I'll say about the girl and her family is that they came from somewhere in the Balkans. Only her father claims, if you can believe him, to have been born in Kosovo. The girl herself had never been to Kosovo."

"That makes it even more rough on the girl."

"What else can they, can she, expect after five years?"

"There is also the manner of arresting her, on a school outing, in sight and hearing of the other kids."

"Don't get me wrong, I do have sympathy for the girl."

The woman interjected, "I have a son who's sixteen, still at school."

"I still maintain," said the man, "that the girl does not belong to Kosovo. She didn't come from Kosovo."

At this point, the woman introduced herself. "I came from Cuba."

The man said, "The best thing about Cuba is the women!"

There was general laughter. I raised my glass to the woman who rose with her drink to clink glasses, the man joined in.

I said, "I come from England."

The man repaid my appreciation of his French by complimenting me on mine. "If you come to Kosovo, you will be treated like a king. They won't be able to do enough for you since you helped us in our darkest days," he added.

I enquired, "How are things there now?"

"Everything's fine. There is no problem. We have our country and no bother."

"Do you not have the bother of the little Serb enclave of Mitrovicia?"

"No, no, Mitrovicia is not Serb. It is divided in half with a bridge straddling them – Kosovar on one side, Serb on the other. They are the losers, lost most of Yugoslavia; their fault for putting their trust in Russia, which is run by the mafia."

"They, in turn, point to your mafia," I said.

"We have no mafia. We have a few criminals, and what country doesn't? Every day millions of euros' worth of drugs pass through Marseilles, yet you read nothing about that. Instead, there is all that talk about some small Kosovo criminals dealing with small quantities; an insult to all of those who work hard and honestly for their living."

The woman interjected again, "*Je fais la cuisine*. What's the food like in England?"

"Not as good as the French," I replied, "but not as bad as the French allege."

"You drink the beer and eat, how do you say it, the Yorkshire pudding," she said.

"If you go to Kosovo, they will put before you whatever you fancied. Particularly if you mention Tony Blair," said the man.

"Would you not like to visit England?" I asked.

"We may do it one day," said the man.

"Perhaps after the honeymoon," added the woman with a smile.

"Congratulations! I wish you all the happiness."

"It will be on the sixteenth of November," she said excitedly.

"With a party to follow," he added.

"The ceremony will be at the *mairie*," she said.

"You may guess," he said, "how riotous the party will be afterwards, a mix of Cubans and Kosovars."

"It will be so lovely!" she said.

The man said, "Bill Clinton and Madeleine Albright, they also helped us, like Tony Blair."

I asked the woman, "Do you have any family in France?"

"I have my mother, a sister and a brother."

"What about your father?"

"I have no father."

The man said, "I wanted my mother to come to the wedding. She wouldn't. She said she was old and frail. Besides, there would have been the problem with the visa."

"My cousin is coming over for the wedding. He was given a visa. His name is Renard, which sounds so funny in French," she said.

"We lived in a small village, not far from Pristina. It was destroyed in the war. We lost everything," he said.

The woman said to me, "I see you ordered *poulpe á la plancha*, a good choice."

The man added, "I have to watch my weight. I ask you, do you think I'm overweight? She made me lose two kilos in one month."

"I want him to look good for the wedding," said the woman.

"My cousin was engaged to be married. Then the war started, and we all took to the hills," he said before suddenly getting up with a jerky movement and walking out.

The woman came across to take his seat closer to me. "Sometimes he has nightmares," she offered. "He is very gentle. A good man. My mother isn't very religious, I not at all. Mother told me he is the best thing that has ever happened to me."

"Yes, he strikes me as *un brave homme*. It shows how much you're both in love."

"He is a proud Slav and doesn't show it as we Cubans do. But he loves me deeply, the same as I love him. He's also a brilliant builder. He can build anything, big or small."

"It would be good to have your email in case we need any work carried out on our *coproprietēe*," I said.

The man returned smelling of cigarette. He took the seat the woman had previously occupied, but she insisted that he resume his old seat next to me. She told him that I had an apartment and would call on him if I needed any work. He said he would do any work big or small. The woman repeated that he was brilliant; there was nothing he couldn't do. He said he gained his expertise from the rebuilding of their homestead and village after the war.

The woman said, "I was a *danseuse* before, but I'm glad I gave that up. For one thing I'm now forty, and I didn't like the men's attentions."

I asked the man if he worked on his own. He said he worked *á la pige*, one job at a time, and was paid when the work was done.

The woman added, "He's brilliant, he can do anything."

"I'm never out of work. We may not be rich, but we'll always have enough," said the man.

"That, and our love. Who would want more?" she said.

"I wouldn't swap it for all those yachts you see over there," he said.

"What time is the wedding?" I asked.

"Eleven, will you come?" the woman replied with excitement.

"I'm returning to England in two days."

"I would so much like you to come," she said.

"And to join us for the celebration afterwards. I was joking when I said it would be riotous. Riotous, perhaps; but not rough," stated the man.

Again, I offered my excuses. Then the woman said as she pointed to a block of flats, "We live over there. Next time you're here, after the wedding and the honeymoon, you come to visit and I'll cook you a nice dish."

"And perhaps one day we come to England and take English tea with you," he said.

The woman enquired about the size of my apartment and said, "Ours is forty-six square metres. It has a big sitting room." She added that her partner could carve out another small bedroom if need be, which has an old fireplace and sea view. "Do you intend to stay there for long?" I asked the woman.

"It's big enough for now. In time, and if we're lucky, we may have to look for a larger one."

"I cried when I saw our village torched. We were in the hills, but there wasn't much we could do to protect ourselves, our homes, our village," said the man.

"If you can manage to come to the wedding, you will see my family and cousin Renard. He's a teacher in Havana," she said.

"Then I saw the helicopters overhead. I was so excited. I called my cousin on his mobile. I told him, 'We are saved; NATO is here,'" he resumed.

"I told you about Renard, my cousin. His sister Esmeralda is married to a doctor. I was at their wedding," said the woman.

We got down to exchanging email addresses. As we had neither pen nor notepaper between us, the woman got them from the waiter and wrote with a neat hand.

The man said, "It's been such a pleasure meeting you. Give our regards to Tony Blair. There are so many streets named after him. Bill Clinton the same, and Madeleine Albright. I was in the company of Hashimi when he received her telephone call on his mobile. She told him the war was over and the terms that had been agreed. We jumped for joy, and I cried with happiness."

"I have never felt so happy. If only you would come to the wedding. I shall be doing much of the cooking. But not the cake. I'll leave that to the expert," said the woman.

I turned to the man and asked, "Are you working tomorrow?"

"Yes, I start early."

The woman said, "I'm taking the day off. I have an appointment with the hairdresser, the one who'll be doing my hair for the wedding."

"That tells you all you need to know. We work to bring in the money, and they spend it on hairdos," he said with a smile.

I raised my glass to the woman and offered, "You do know the English expression 'She's worth it.'"

They collapsed with laughter.

"I am so very, very happy," she said, beaming.

The man said, "When I was a lad, my father said to me, 'You will grow to be a man and will then have to build a home.'"

The woman said, "You can do anything. One day you will build a house, if you wanted."

The man leaned forward over the table, took hold of both her hands with more tenderness than he had shown until then. "My darling, beautiful Cuban Leydiana, I shall build us a house one day, a good strong house, you just wait and see. But that wasn't quite what Father meant."

As we rose to take our leave, the man shook me firmly by the hand and said, "Don't be surprised if we come one day to take tea with you in England."

The woman, after the conventional two kisses, said, "Try to come to our wedding. Don't forget the date, the sixteenth of November, eleven o'clock, *la mairie*!"

* * *

The Bar

You ask, as you contemplate a career in law, what it is like to be a barrister. There's no simple answer to that question. The Bar is a great profession: engaging intellectually, challenging morally and, yes, it can be rewarding materially. But life at the Bar is hard work. It can cause anxiety, bouts of self-doubt and insecurity – insecurity most of all. You can go three days without work and think it's the end of your career, so you get up on the fourth contemplating transitioning to a solicitor or joining the Crown Prosecution Service, or giving up law altogether and retraining as a teacher. Then you walk into chambers, look in your pigeonhole and there's a new set of instructions. You're back in business! The gloom is lifted, your spirits are lifted – you're excited.

This feeling lasts until you undo the red tape, find a case that's badly prepared, a difficult client who will give you grief, a modest fee that you'll wait a long time to receive, if at all, and counsel is asked to use his or her best endeavours to push along a speculative claim or vindicate a desperate defence. That's what it's like to be a barrister. But not entirely, for when you do a good job, when you feel that you've made a difference, when you have the pleasure of arguing a nice point of law, and when you have the singular privilege of participating in however small way in pushing the boundaries of the law, see your name in a reported case, the case in a textbook, there are not many other feelings that could compare.

One fundamental characteristic in the practice of law is uncertainty. No two courts, nor two court days, nor two cases are the same. No matter how well and carefully you prepare your case, no matter how meritorious it is on its facts and in the law applicable to it, you cannot be fully confident of the outcome; particularly so before knowing the name and idiosyncrasies of the judge who will be trying it, the name and general repute of your opposing advocate and the quality of your witnesses. And there's always the risk of the unexpected emerging in the course of a trial that will set it on a different course: new evidence of which you had no knowledge or a new development in the law of which you were unaware.

A day in the life of a barrister is often the death walk from car park to courthouse, and the euphoric or sombre walk from courthouse to car park. Yet you can never have enough of it. I would describe it the way an oriental medieval scribe once described a daily life in the court of the caliphs: it is like a *hammam,* a bathhouse; when you are inside feeling the heat you want to get out, but once outside you can hardly wait to go back in.

Another fundamental characteristic of the practice of the law is its diversity; it runs the full gamut of human experience. At one end it can be the drama of a criminal prosecution or the theatre of a libel trial, and at the other end low-key hearings such as a licensing or planning application, a property or matrimonial dispute. As a barrister, your practice is confined to a small part or parts of that kaleidoscope.

The law is dynamic, changing all the time while every decided case stands to define it even as it strains to nudge its boundaries. Taking divorce as an example, there was a time when divorce petitions were not entirely devoid of the dramatic and theatrical, reports of some such filling the newsprint. But this has almost disappeared by the time you sit down to read this. A marriage can now be dissolved by consent after a period of waiting or otherwise due to one of the parties demonstrating by one means or another that the marriage is no longer viable. What then remains in contention is the clearing up of the consequences of that dissolution including the claim and cross-claims over maintenance and property. This is normally conducted in the privacy of the judge's chambers away from the glare of publicity. The inquiry agent, who in the past served to obtain the newsworthy notorious evidence to support the divorce petition, is now replaced by the forensic sleuthing to prove the existence or otherwise of the parties' respective assets, means and needs.

Rare is the property dispute that isn't overlain by deep emotions, feelings of guilt and bitterness. The dispute over every item of the matrimonial assets recalls the memory of its acquisition, the how and the when, the discussion surrounding its acquisition, the how paid for and by whom, and, most of all, the then state of the marriage. Every memory evokes the regret of dreams denied and hopes let slip, and the bitter ripples of the shortcomings that cannot be admitted, the daily hurts that cannot be repaired and, as in the case of Robert (not his real name), the infidelity that cannot be forgiven.

Robert was a man of substance, in his early sixties when I first met him as a client, the scion of a long-established Yorkshire family and head of a midsized steel factory that had been founded by his great-grandfather. As he grew up, his world was the factory, the family home close by and the church he attended on a Sunday, whose yard was the last resting place of generations of his ancestors. He was an only child and when his father died, he replaced him as head of the business and, in a sense, head of the family. There were several relatives who owned shares in the business, passed down to them through inheritance. Robert knew all there was to know about the business. He ran it cautiously and profitably, which allowed him to maintain the yearly dividend that the shareholders counted on. He worked full-time, attended the factory every day and went home at the midday break to lunch with his mother.

He kept to the same routine when his mother died, except that he now sat all alone at the dinner table to have lunch prepared by a daily help. He had no outside interests other than the membership of a local chess club where he would spend Thursday evenings and the occasional going by invitation to watch a county cricket match. He had the natural desire a healthy, lusty man would have for womanly love and the longing for female company, particularly after the death of his mother. But the reserve and sobriety of his daily existence and routine left no room for romantic entanglement. That was to change after he met Rosina, Rosa for short.

For a long time the business relied on the accountancy services of a local accountant. Then his practice was taken over by a leading London firm. That was soon followed by Rosa visiting to establish contact. Robert showed her around the factory and office, explained the business and in general terms the accountancy system in place, took her to the local public house for lunch, and then they returned to the office for a further discussion.

It was a successful visit. Robert was happy and proud to discuss his business and its success, and he was as charmed by Rosa's attentiveness as impressed by her knowledge and professionalism, particularly after she indicated that, with the backing of her people in London, she would come up with some tax saving ideas. Rosa also warmed to Robert and was pleased to have his business allocated to her as a special client. The first visit was followed by others.

On the third visit, they had lunch at his house. By the end of the year, they were married.

They were well suited. Rosa was ten years younger than Robert, a widow with an unmarried daughter in her twenties living in Brighton. Rosa had her own flat in London on mortgage with a little loan outstanding and she had a good job. But while she was reasonably well-off, independent and financially secure, she thought with dismay at the prospect of living alone for the rest of her days. Marrying Robert answered all her requirements and stilled all anxieties, and she was genuinely fond of him. She sold her London flat, moved to Robert's house and accompanied him most days to the factory where she took charge of the accounts and office administration.

To Robert it was a marriage made in heaven: a wife he doted on and a partner who was a great help in the running of the business, which became even more successful as a result. And there were profound changes in the way he viewed the world. He blossomed emotionally, gave up chess and, looking in the mirror every morning, he would now see a happy, contended, successful and good-looking man. He began to take more care of his appearance and show more interest in women generally, and he felt that his unspoken interest was at times met by unspoken reciprocal approval. He also became more confident socially. Over the years he received many social and business invitations, which he always turned down. But now when he received an invitation from the Institute of Directors for a two-day seminar in London, he discussed it with his wife who was in favour. He thought he would enjoy it; she reasoned that it would be an opportunity for some useful networking.

He happened to have a seat at the seminar next to Anne-Louise. They introduced themselves to each other and exchanged observations about the government and the economy; this continued while they were served drinks during the interval. In the evening, they were surprised to discover that they were staying at the same gentleman's club.

The following day they attended the seminar as lovers. During the following six months there were occasions when

Robert found reasons to go down to London, as did Anne-Louise whose home was in Bristol. Rosa was eventually alerted to the goings-on by the details in a monthly statement of the business credit card. She confronted her husband who confessed. But he assured her that she was still the only love in his life, promised to have no further contact with the other woman and asked her to forgive him.

Rosa took what she considered a betrayal very badly. She packed her bags, went to live with her daughter, and lost no time in seeing a solicitor and then issuing a petition for divorce on the grounds of her husband's adultery. Robert did not contest the petition while continuing to plead with Rosa to reconsider her position and give the marriage another chance. That cut no ice with Rosa's obduracy. A decree nisi was pronounced, followed by the hearing of Rosa's application for a property adjustment order before the decree absolute. I was instructed to represent Robert at the hearing.

As a court hearing, it was not challenging. It had been agreed before I became involved that the combined assets of the parties, other than Robert's shares in the business, some held in trust, be divided equally. Nor were there any grounds to dispute the other, matrimonial, assets; Rosa had full knowledge of every item.

She had prepared two schedules for the court hearing, one listing her own assets and the other listing Robert's. Both schedules were confirmed and approved by Robert. The rest of the hearing was taken up by Rosa proposing how the agreed terms could be efficiently implemented, with a particular eye on the tax implications. Robert was full of admiration for Rosa and accepted all that she proposed without demur. His concern even at that stage was to save the marriage; hence, he was prepared to do anything that would mollify his wife. He would not accept that deep down she couldn't bring herself to forgive his infidelity, a temporary lapse, nor accept that through lasting bitterness she would put an end to what he perceived to be a happy and successful marriage. He attributed her obduracy to the nefarious influence of her daughter who had objected to the marriage in the first place and never quite got on with him thereafter. In the event, Robert's delusional hope was dashed; a court order was issued embodying the agreed terms for equal division. The decree absolute soon followed.

The brief came back to me three years later in exceptional circumstances. Rosa had died in the meantime, the daughter saw to the funeral and burial in a plot of land that Rosa had indicated to her. Now a dispute over the plot's ownership had arisen. It appeared that Robert and Rosa had discussed what arrangements to leave in place for their funerals during the course of the marriage. It was out of the question for Rosa's mortal remains to join Robert's in the churchyard. That didn't appeal to her. Besides, she was of a different faith nominally and secular by conviction. Since it was their desire to be together in death as in life, they bought a plot in a humanist garden of rest in Derbyshire. It was a double plot in two halves; Rosa's remains were now resting in one half. Still grieving over his loss, Robert would visit the grave and leave a bunch of flowers. Then he arranged for two identical trees to be planted, one on each half of the plot. The daughter, visiting the grave on the anniversary of her mother's birthday, was surprised to see the trees and then irate when told they had been planted by Robert.

A few days later, Robert received a letter from a Brighton solicitor accusing him of trespass and warning him to keep his hands off Rosa's grave and his person at a distance from the plot. That was answered by Robert pointing out that he was the owner of the plot, or at least the half of it that will be his final resting place. The daughter countered that her mother had been so badly affected by Robert's betrayal that she would not have wanted him to be buried next to her. Further, relying on the discussion she'd had with her mother as to what the latter wanted for her funeral, which included burial in *her* plot, she reasoned that it must have been taken into account in the divorce settlement and allocated to Rosa as part of her half share. This was the immediate reason for the brief being returned to me. I pointed out that as far as I recalled no mention was made of the plot at the hearing. The other counsel who acted for Rosa said the same. Copies of the two property schedules were obtained from the court registry; there was no mention of the plot in either schedule.

The incontestable conclusion was that with so many major assets considered, a small plot of land of insignificant monetary value was simply overlooked. The daughter then pointed to the fact that her mother was an accountant, thorough in all she did, who took great care over details. She suggested that the only explanation for the omission of the plot from the schedules would have been that her mother had paid for it and so acquired it as her own sole property and which, given the illusory monetary value, she saw no reason to have it included.

In order to resolve that argument, a joint approach was made to the administrators of the garden. A search of their records disclosed that the sale had been made to Robert and Rosa as joint purchasers, payment by cheque drawn on their joint bank account. The search also revealed that the double plot they had purchased was other than the one in which Rosa was now buried; her mortal remains rested in another couple's plot destined for their own burial in the future. The mistake had been the result of a confusion in the numbering of plots not then defined physically on the ground. The garden's owners were contrite and offered to do all they could to rectify the situation.

Rosa's daughter was now hysterical and threatened to have her mother's body exhumed and reburied near her in Brighton. Robert, horrified at that prospect, sought out the other couple, bought the plot off them, which he then ceded to the daughter on condition that no part of it be used by anyone or for any purpose other than Rosa's resting place. In return, Rosa's daughter was prevailed upon to abandon whatever claim she might have had over the other double plot.

In due course, Robert would have the satisfaction of it being his own resting place, not adjoining Rosa's, but in the same garden; the two separated by a canopy of trees, so as spring turned to summer and summer to autumn, and the trees became bare of flowers and leaves, each would be in sight of the other.

❊ ❊ ❊

Unmeritorious

As a barrister, you are often asked how you could bring yourself to stand up in court to argue a case that is patently unmeritorious. One answer is that you have no choice in the matter. The Bar works mostly on the cab-rank principle; you cannot refuse to do a case because you do not like it. You would certainly prefer to be fighting for one that had merits, the better the prospects of success the more acceptable. As you stand up to argue a case that is of little merit, you expose yourself to the derision of your opposing advocate and the cruel jibes of the judge addressed to you personally, since they cannot be addressed to your client who may be absent from the court or sitting behind shielded by you as his representative and mouthpiece. Furthermore, and no matter how unmeritorious the case is, or intrinsically hopeless, its failure would still be marked as your loss. That said, rare is the case so unmeritorious as to leave you tongue-tied while you felt duty-bound to try to vindicate it.

Ronald Turnbull was a widower in his eighties, living on his own in Bradford. He had two daughters: Jenny, twice divorced, who lived quite near in Pudsey; and Jennifer who was single and lived and worked in Brussels. He had made a will leaving them his estate in equal shares. The estate consisted of his house and a small amount of savings in the bank. The will was silent as to the destination of the house contents, which were of modest value. There were a few desirable objects, the rest consisted of furniture and utensils of everyday use. The daughters saw the creeping frailty of their father and each secretly speculated what would happen to the contents when he died. Jenny had her eye on the pictures in particular, including a pair of oils on canvas signed "Marcus" depicting Maidenhead Bridge and *The Complete Angler*. They reminded her of her first honeymoon. Jennifer had her eye on a set of Waterford crystal cups, which hadn't been touched since they were received by Mr and Mrs Turnbull as a wedding present some fifty years before. And the daughters each coveted the gold-rimmed Wedgwood tea service that had been used twice in the course of their parents' marriage, then kept proudly in a glass-fronted display cabinet in the front reception room.

Jenny was of an anxious disposition besides being inordinately greedy; her anxiety and greed were heightened by the story of her friend Francis. The latter was on holiday in Thailand when her widowed mother died. She missed the funeral and by the time she got back, her siblings had virtually emptied the mother's home, shared the contents and hadn't left Francis a single object of value or sentimental worth. Jenny was determined to avoid such a fate.

Then Ronald had a stroke. He was rushed to hospital where he recovered consciousness, but then he had another attack leaving him comatose. Jenny wasted no time in calling a removal company who cleared the contents of his house leaving it with bare walls, threadbare carpets and old curtains on the ground floor. The contents were mostly transferred to Jenny's house, some of the large pieces replacing hers that were shabbier. What was left of little worth or surplus to requirements in both houses was disposed of by sale to a house-clearing merchant or otherwise thrown away. The task completed, Jenny sat herself down on the newly acquired old familiar sofa, lit a cigarette and picked up the telephone.

Jennifer flew over as soon as she received the grave news about their father. After going to the hospital and then to her father's house, she was outraged to see the state of affairs and went to challenge her sister. A big argument ensued, but Jenny was in no way discomfited. She said that she was entitled to do what she did. She alleged that she'd had a discussion with their father a few days before he was taken ill, that she happened to mention how much she liked the Marcus paintings. He allegedly told her to treat all there was in the house as hers; he may have had a premonition of imminent death. Unsurprisingly, Jennifer didn't believe a word of that. She accused Jenny of lying and stealing, said no one could believe Jenny's story of Ronald allegedly giving away in his lifetime the furniture he used, including the very sofa on which he reclined and the very bed in which he slept.

The argument became heated, some unpleasant unsisterly words were exchanged, threats of retribution and curses were flung about, and Jennifer went to see a solicitor. But there was no easy legal remedy. If Jenny had committed trespass and wrongful misappropriation of goods, the aggrieved party was Ronald; Jennifer had no personal claim or other standing in the matter. In normal circumstances, it might have been possible to persuade Ronald to start legal proceedings, much that he would have been reluctant to do so against Jenny, his daughter. But these were not normal circumstances: Ronald was in no position to do anything being comatose. So Jennifer would have to institute the lawsuit herself in his name and for his benefit, and to have the conduct of the proceedings as in effect his agent. But that was not without difficulty, nor could one say if Ronald would approve of such a course were he able to know what was being proposed.

However, those complications were resolved, and in the most dramatic fashion. Ronald suddenly – and against all expectations – came out of the coma, regained consciousness and said he wanted to go home. He was then informed that he no longer had a usable home. Apprised of how it came to pass that he had lost the contents he, egged on by Jennifer, started an action against Jenny. The action followed its normal course and a date was set for the court hearing. I was briefed to appear for Jenny and to use my best endeavours to defeat the claim.

I had a conference with Jenny before the start of the hearing. She was in a state of high agitation. She kept on saying that she would never allow *them* to carry away *her* furniture. She expected me to protect her from what would be a terrible injustice; she complained bitterly of the traitor, the snake in the grass, living immorally in Brussels and now come to cause her mischief. She had sympathy for her father, but there was no doubt that he was being manipulated and lied to. He was then in a nursing home, incapable of appearing in court in person, so a court official called on him and obtained a statement to be read in court as his testimony. Jenny would not accept the accuracy of the statement, nor the validity of the signature said to be his. I then felt relief when looking at the clock and noting that it was time to go into court, but I was surprised to see two reporters whom I knew and more people in the public section than you would usually expect to see on any normal day in Bradford county court. News of the dispute had apparently been mentioned in the local newspaper.

I thought my best course was to mostly leave it to Jenny to state her own case, for her to explain and justify. She showed herself fully up to the task. For a start she pointed to her closeness to her parents over the years, her mother in particular for whom she acted as carer during her last illness and attended to her needs every day. She contrasted this with Jennifer's indifference, that she was a disappointment to the family and barely visited while living it up in Brussels. Coming to the main issue, after a long and bitter preamble, Jenny said that one day as she helped her mother out of bed and then started to clean, her mother had told her everything in the house would be hers. Reminded that she had given a different account of the incident when she alleged it had been her father who made the promise, she stressed vehemently that it had been the mother's, later confirmed by the father.

Jenny still had to deal with a major hurdle, which was her taking possession of the house contents while her father was still alive. She dealt with this by alleging, at variance with her earlier evidence, that she was to have them when he no longer required them. Her final plea was that it would be cruel to allow him to go back home at his age and disability, that he only started the proceedings under the evil influence of Jennifer, and then added with a flourish, "It is criminal to force him to go home. Who will be there to look after him? Will she come back to look after him?"

The judge listened patiently to Jenny, didn't allow any interruptions, complimented her for the clear and controlled manner by which she had given her evidence in what were very trying circumstances, and then gave judgement against her.

Jenny now lost her poise completely. As the judge rose and turned away, she screamed, "Do you call this English justice?" She was still protesting loudly as I ushered her out of the courtroom, shielded her from the attention of the reporters and guided her to a quiet corner where I tried to calm her down. She now turned her venom on me saying I had done nothing to help and, in particular, failed to point out that what purported to be Ronald Turnbull's signature on her father's alleged statement was a forgery. A woman came to comfort her, I assumed a friend or neighbour. That gave me the chance to slip away.

Back in chambers, the clerk saw the dried perspiration on my face as I saw the dismay on his.

"I know, I know," I said before he could say anything. "Second loser in two days!"

"Never mind, we win some, we lose some," he said. "Your luck's bound to turn. Here's your brief for tomorrow, a nice little earner, interesting easy case – a neighbours' dispute over a hedge."

* * *

Alvin

Yesterday I had occasion to look again at Kafka's *The Trial*. I first read it in my student days many years ago. Looking at it now has brought back to me the case of Alvin White. Like Kafka's protagonist, Alvin got up in all innocence early one morning and found himself in a vortex of incomprehensible events: arrest, accusation, criminal investigation, murder charge, incarceration and a succession of court appearances culminating in a trial. His case is also an object lesson in the pitfalls of criminal investigations and proceedings.

Gillside House was an imposing property that once graced Roker seafront in Sunderland. But at the time of the events here described, it stood derelict after years of waiting to be demolished. It became notorious as the haunt of tramps, drug users, alcohol abusers, glue sniffers, as well as young persons looking for mischief or to engage in more innocent activities. One day, shortly after his fifteenth birthday, the schoolboy Alvin White and his then girlfriend, two years his junior, went to Gillside House and had sex on an old mattress in an alcove. They were both sexually active, so that episode would not have registered with either of them as particularly distinguishable from similar activities they had shared with each other and others respectively.

A year later, Simon Martin's semi-clad body was found on that mattress. He had been battered to death. He was fourteen years old. The police forensic investigators looked for clues in the alcove. Their attention was drawn to a particular stain on the wall close to the body. They thought it was a bloodstain, but one could not be certain as blood, seen as crimson when shed, fades to other shades with the passage of time. Further, in order to obtain better details of the stain, they treated it with a solution of ninhydrin. That yielded the details of a human fingerprint, but in the process affected the material and rendered it beyond reliable identification as blood.

Simon Martin and Alvin went to the same school, so the police obtained fingerprints from all the pupils. Alvin's matched that in the alcove.

Alvin was alone at home when they arrested him, predawn; his parents were away on holiday. As he opened the front door, a posse of non-uniformed officers barged in. While the senior officer, Detective Richard Hall, questioned him, others went through the house searching for anything that might incriminate him, of which there was nothing. Hall, without indicating the reason for his question, asked Alvin if he had ever been inside Gillside House, to which Alvin replied that he hadn't. This patent lie registered with the policeman as an important piece of evidence in the case that was to be assembled.

In reality, it was nothing of the sort. Over the years, scores of men would have been inside the house; they were all trespassers engaged in nefarious activities of different degrees of gravity. If Hall had posed the same question out of the blue to any one of them, he in all likelihood would have received the same response. Next, Alvin was taken to the scene of the crime. Accused of lying as he was shown what they said was his fingerprint on the wall, he admitted that his earlier denial was false; he now remembered that some twelve months before he'd had sex there with a girlfriend whom he now named. Whereupon, Alvin was taken to the police station and confined in a cell with a total ban on outside contact lest he managed to communicate with the girl before the police had interviewed her. In the event, she was interviewed in the presence of her grandmother. She said she knew Alvin but denied that she'd ever had sex with him at Gillside House.

Hall saw this as a very significant part of the evidential case that was emerging, but it is worth observing that at no time during the course of that interview was the girl told that it related in any way to the murder inquiry.

There followed an intensive questioning of Alvin designed to break his resistance and make him admit to the crime. At first, his father was allowed to be present. But while Alvin was cool and unflustered throughout, his father was emotional as he supported his son, often interrupting the questioning and objecting to what he perceived to be the aggressive manner and unfairness in which it was conducted. After a few sessions, the father was excluded and barred from ever being present at the interviews. But what struck Hall most forcibly was the demeanour of Alvin. He displayed no emotion, expressed no regret, showed no anxiety as he was led inside Gillside House, no horror as he was made to stand in the alcove and be shown the place where the victim's body was discovered, and no sense of pity for the victim who was known to him as a fellow student. Hall, who'd had a lot of experience in dealing with suspects and criminals, judged Alvin to be a calm, cool and heartless killer. He might have reconsidered that judgement if he had been aware that Alvin suffered habitually from an apparent lack of emotional response and difficulty expressing his feelings; he had in fact a condition bordering on the autistic.

As the period of holding Alvin in police custody before a charge was limited by law, Hall took the decision to charge him with murder while continuing the criminal investigation.

Appearing in court, Alvin's application for bail was successfully opposed by the police on the grounds that to allow him freedom would prejudice the investigation. In the course of that hearing, the court was informed of the fingerprint as a principal plank in the prosecution case, as well as Alvin's rebuttal based on his account of sexual intercourse with a girl some time before the murder. The report of that hearing came to the notice of the girl who then went to the police and confirmed Alvin's account. Hall was not satisfied with the girl's change of evidence. He held on to the belief that the girl's initial denial was true, so that the change might have been an attempt by the girl, of her own volition or under inducement, to assist Alvin by providing him with a false alibi. Hall asked the girl if she had been menstruating when she was engaged in the alleged sexual intercourse. She said that she was not. Hall saw that as undermining the defence since it was inconsistent with an innocent explanation for Alvin's admitted fingerprint on the wall of the alcove, which the police took to have been made in blood. If the blood did not come from the girl, then Alvin's fingerprint must have been made in Simon Martin's blood. Yet the flaw in that proposition was obvious: there was no incontrovertible evidence that the print was made in blood. Furthermore, there could hardly have been any evidential value in asking a sexually active young girl if she had been menstruating on one particular occasion a year before, and putting reliance on the assumed veracity of the answer.

The investigation continued without yielding any other clues. All attempts to extract a DNA from the fingerprint ended in failure and successive bail applications were dismissed. Restrictions were imposed on Alvin's contact with his family. A probation officer was assigned to look after him. The probation officer reported a strange occurrence. He said that one day Alvin suddenly had a bad turn in his presence, went white in the face, made fists, screwed his eyes, went all rigid and exclaimed, "I will not do it again!" That was reported to Hall who took it to be an admission of guilt. The probation officer then turned that report into a formal witness statement to form part of the prosecution case at trial.

When, sometime later, Alvin's lawyers asked him to comment on that statement, he said he had no recollection of the alleged incident. But even taking the report at face value, it is difficult to see much value in it forensically. What was it that Alvin would not do again?

After the investigation had dragged on for five months, a review was carried out by the prosecution which involved, in addition to Hall, a representative of the Crown Prosecution Service and a leading barrister. They concluded that a conviction was unlikely on the evidence available. In arriving at that conclusion, they were influenced by the fact that what connected Alvin to the murder was a single fingerprint. If he had been the killer, he would have likely left more telltale marks in blood. The prosecution was discontinued, the charge dropped and Alvin was set free. He had spent five months in custody.

But trouble didn't end there for Alvin and his family. The dropping of the charge and not being acquitted by a jury did little to rehabilitate his reputation. In the eyes of many, he was a killer. He was beaten up in Sunderland city centre shortly after his release by a group of youths chanting "murderer". He was shunned by men and women of his generation. He could not get a job until his father, who was highly regarded where he worked, got him a junior job in the same company. And his family felt it badly. They never doubted Alvin's innocence yet carried a heavy burden since his arrest. The matter was in the back of their minds all the time. If people looked at them whenever they went out, they assumed they were being seen as the family of a murderer. They and Alvin felt that he was denied a trial that would have cleared his name. When he turned eighteen, he offered to stand trial for the murder. An offer that the authorities turned down.

The burden did not become any lighter with the passage of time. Alvin and his family continued looking for ways to finally clear his name. Eventually, Alvin was advised that he could only hope to achieve this by suing the police authority for false imprisonment and malicious prosecution. In order to succeed in that claim, Alvin would have to satisfy the court that he was innocent of the accusation and charge of murder. Hence, winning the proposed action would constitute a formal exoneration in addition to an award of compensation. At the same time Alvin was advised of the risk, in that the withdrawal of the charge, unlike acquittal after a trial, still left him in jeopardy; he could still be made to face the charge of murder. Alvin, notwithstanding the misgivings of his family, was willing to run that risk.

But the contemplated action would incur substantial costs. Alvin could only undertake this with the support of public funds. He made an application for legal aid, but this was rejected by the legal aid administrators because the claim was not sufficiently meritorious. That decision was upheld by the local committee of the legal aid board. At that stage a new lawyer took up the case, and the decision was carried on appeal to a higher tribunal and reversed; so with the benefit of legal aid, the action was commenced and a statement of claim lodged on behalf of Alvin.

The police authority's response was to apply to the court to have the action dismissed because it had to be shown that Alvin was acquitted of murder for such a claim to be sustained, and that the dropping of the charge did not constitute an acquittal. This was tried as a preliminary issue and resulted in the judgement that the dropping of the charge and discontinuance of criminal proceedings were sufficient to sustain the claim.

Alvin was allowed to proceed in his action against the police authority. The latter filed a defence that went beyond alleging that they acted in good faith on the evidence as they saw it, which asserted that there were, and continued to be, good grounds for the murder accusation.

Undeterred, Alvin continued with the action and in due course applied, as he was entitled in law, for the case to be tried by judge and jury. The police opposed that and sought to limit it to trial by judge alone. This important procedural point was argued before a senior judge who, in disregard of Alvin's right in the matter, ordered that the case be tried by judge alone, and a date was set for the trial. The reason the judge gave for his decision was that a jury trial would last longer, it would be more costly and would take up more valuable court time. That order was taken to the Court of Appeal which, while expressing sympathy for Alvin, upheld the order on the practical grounds, as they saw them, that to reverse it and substitute a jury trial would involve the relisting of the trial date with further costs and delay which would not be in Alvin's best interest!

The day before the commencement of the trial, the police disclosed that they had obtained a DNA from the fingerprint – it was a full match for the girl. The explanation given for the late disclosure was that due to the imminence of the trial, a new attempt was made to obtain the DNA, which succeeded due to alleged "new and improved" procedures. That was a complete exoneration of Alvin. The only remaining issue now at the trial was whether the police authority was liable in damages.

Alvin and his family had the satisfaction of seeing Detective Superintendent Richard Hall, now retired, appear in court to admit that there was not a shred of evidence linking Alvin White to the murder of Simon Martin, and express his sympathy to Alvin and his family. It was argued for Alvin that, in the absence of any such evidence, his arrest and being held in custody for five months amounted to malice in the legal sense of the term. In the event, the trial judge was not persuaded to make such a finding against the police. Instead, he directed that consideration be given by the Home Office to compensate Alvin with an ex gratia payment, which he received in due course. Alvin and his family had the greater satisfaction of seeing the full report of the trial in the media and full front-page coverage in the leading local newspaper under the bold headline "ALVIN IS NO KILLER".

Alvin White was a youth of sixteen when arrested. He was a twenty-six-year-old man at the conclusion of the trial.

* * *

Mr S, Barrister

"When applying for a judicial appointment in England, one is normally required to appear in person before a panel whose task is to enquire into one's competence and suitability for the post by a process of questions and answers. In order to assess the temperament of the applicant and its likely effect on his or her conduct in court, there is often the searching question: what is the one thing more than any other that would make you angry?"

"Another generally accepted convention relating to panegyric, is that the qualities praised should be appropriate to the status and function of the person praised: courage in a military man, fairness in a judge, wisdom in a bureaucrat and modesty in a clerk. Conversely, one should not refer to a bureaucrat as brave, nor to a judge as passionate" (Ibn Rashīq, *The Slave Girls of Baghdad: The Qiyan in the Early Abbasid Era*).

I was in court number one this morning together with many others who were present to hear and participate in the tributes to "S", who died at a relatively young age while in practice as a barrister and part-time judge. He was well liked, by general consent a brilliant advocate and a sound lawyer who came to the Bar with a first-class law degree from Cambridge. He scored near to the top in the Bar examination and was awarded a Harmsworth scholarship. Everyone spoke of his integrity as a lawyer, his fairness as a judge, his loyalty to colleagues as well as his generosity with advice and help to anyone who asked. But the unspoken thought that ran through many was that "S" was an exceptional man who had started his career with a great promise that remained unfulfilled. After a few years in practice, he was appointed an Assistant Recorder, then a Recorder; yet that was to be the limit of his ascent up the judicial ladder.

In the course of my practice at the Bar, I seldom came into contact with "S", ours being no more than a nodding acquaintance since we practised in different areas of the law, he in crime and I in land law and trust. There was just the one case I recall in which we were both involved, he sitting as a member of a panel and I appearing as an advocate, and it was outside the normal ambit of our respective specialities. It was the case of Michelle, tragic on its facts and interesting, meaning difficult, as regards the law. She had the misfortune of being born to a poor, dysfunctional family: a useless father who could not provide, spending whatever money came his way on booze and horse race betting, and a mother who could not cope. They were in receipt of social benefits, yet the larder was often empty by Thursday. The gas company had put them on a coin-operated meter, yet there were many times the food remained uncooked while the last few coins were spent on a packet of cigarettes. Then one day the father, perhaps fuelled by drink, took a saw to the gas pipe attempting to create a diversion to bypass the meter. It resulted in an explosion and a fire that engulfed the house. The mother died in the fire while Michelle, then twelve years old, was rescued but badly burnt. After several operations she was still left badly scarred, the right-hand side of her face shrivelled and right hand deformed. She was taken into the care of the local authority. The father went to prison.

Two years after the fire, by which time the medical treatment had terminated, the care home in which Michelle was living consulted a solicitor who lodged an application on her behalf to the Criminal Injuries Compensation Board seeking an award to compensate her for the injuries. The application went before a single adjudicator who dismissed it on legal grounds. That was when the brief landed on my desk with instructions to represent Michelle and argue her case before a full panel by way of appeal.

The criminal injuries compensation scheme was set up by the government to compensate blameless victims of violent crime who had no recourse to obtain compensation elsewhere. There was no dispute of the facts in Michelle's case. She had suffered a grievous injury and loss of which she was blameless. They were the result of a crime committed by her father with deliberate, dishonest intent. There was no prospect of her recovering compensation from him as the wrongdoer. But that still left a serious consideration and stumbling block: was Michelle the victim of a "violent" crime?

I was struck by Michelle's appearance when I first saw her outside the boardroom where the appeal was to be heard. If you could have ignored the obvious disfigurement, you would have seen an attractive girl who looked even younger than her fourteen years: pure milk-white complexion, shoulder-length golden tresses and bright blue eyes. She rarely lifted her face and otherwise kept it turned to the right, to present the unblemished side to view, and she covered her right hand with the left. I was also struck by her demeanour. She displayed no emotion meeting me for the first time as her advocate, nor at being where we were, nor any anxiety about her appeal. In fact, she impressed me as unnaturally passive, the passivity of one who is used to one's fate being determined by others whose decisions one accepted unquestioningly.

The demeanour did not change as we were admitted to the boardroom, which was set up as a formal tribunal for the day. There was the panel of adjudicators seated at a long table facing a solitary chair for me as advocate while Michelle was seated on one of the chairs ranged against the wall. The panel consisted of the chairman and two wing members, Mr S, as the more junior, seated to the left of the chairman.

I saw the name-card in front of the chairman and identified him as a formidable lawyer, a very senior, perhaps then the most senior, member of the Board, with a lifetime of experience in the law and practice of the criminal injuries compensation scheme. He had taken part in drawing it up and in the campaign to get it on the statute book. It occurred to me that he may have reserved our appeal to himself because of its legal interest. As I deployed my arguments, I could sense his mischievous pleasure at knocking them down one after another. Michelle's claim was unsustainable if one simply took the facts at face value, that is of the girl's injuries being the result of her father's dishonesty and no more. I had to demonstrate by argument that the sawing of the gas pipe could also be construed as, in effect, an act of pregnant violence. I could see that my arguments were not having much impact; the chairman had the better of the argument and was enjoying it.

When that line of argument was exhausted, the chairman introduced a further element in the case: could an act be categorised as violent within the meaning of the scheme if, as in the case under consideration, the wrongdoer did what he did with no malicious intent or thought of violence towards the victim, his daughter? By that stage, the appeal had transformed into an academic dialectical exercise in which the chairman's arguments prevailed comprehensively, hard though I tried to deflect him from what I perceived to be the inevitable dismissal of the appeal. All the time Michelle sat hunched up in her chair, with the deformed right hand in the firm grip of her left.

But as I attempted another line of argument, which was forthwith countered by the chairman with derision, there was a loud interruption. It was "S", the left-wing member, who raised a fist and brought it down heavily on the table. "I have had enough," he said loudly. "I can't bear it any longer!" He made to rise, but the chairman turned and held him by the sleeve and persuaded him to settle down. The stunned silence was then broken by "S" adding passionately by way of explanation, "What is the meaning of all this? What are we doing? Where's our humanity?"

I turned to look at Michelle who had raised her head when she heard the commotion. I saw fear in her face, the face of a simple, institutionalised child who associated the loud shout of an adult in authority as a sign of personal disapproval. Then two tears could be seen sliding down her cheeks. The chairman suspended the hearing momentarily, asked me to retire from the room and to wait outside with the girl for further development.

Some twenty minutes later we were called back. There was total stillness in the room; the tension was palpable. The chairman addressed me softly while the wing members, with eyes fixed straight ahead, were as rigid as statues in their seats. The chairman explained that having heard my arguments they now wanted me to supplement them in writing, which they would then consider without my needing to reappear before them. He added as a parting shot that they wanted me to present the best and strongest arguments I could muster. This was a clear intimation that the appeal would be allowed.

Some years later, I happened to meet my instructing solicitor and we reminisced over the cases of particular interest that we worked on together, and that brought up the case of Michelle. He told me that she was awarded a full compensation; some of the money was then used to pay for corrective plastic surgery. When she was of an age that she had control of her own money as an independent young woman with a place of her own, she attracted the attention of several young men. She fell in love with one who soon frittered away the money and disappeared, leaving her with a child, Edward, on whom she doted. That also happened to be the first name of

"S". I wondered whether the naming of the child was a coincidence or based on informed choice. At any rate it was a happy, well-deserved choice. Edward S, BA Cantab., Harmsworth scholar, brilliant advocate, sound lawyer, Recorder of the Crown Courts, passionate barrister.

As we honour your memory, I salute your humanity.

* * *

Twilight: A Day in the Life of

He was required to be in France to finalise the arrangement for the terrace, so he had to make the travel arrangements at short notice. His son booked him a flight from Liverpool. The son had the flight reference on his computer and was to telephone him on the day of departure to give it to him in case it was required.

He started packing all that was needed. He did that, as he had taught himself to do so, in the order that the stages of the journey would unfold; which he had set out in a list as *aide mémoire* the week before, and consulted several times since: (i) car park voucher (ii) passport and boarding pass at the airport (iii) driving licence for the car hire at destination (iv) 2,90 euros in coins for the autoroute toll (v) keys to the apartment. Also sundries: (a) mobile (b) charger (c) hearing aid (d) medicines (e) change of clothing.

The flight was to be at 10:20. As he was a light sleeper, he woke at 3:00 and then slept fitfully until 5:00 when he got up, looked at the list, checked and rechecked and verified the listed items several times in turn. He left the house at 6:45 after he remembered to take his morning medicine and had verified the list for a final time. Once in the car, he noticed that the petrol tank was only half-full, which had been missed off the list. There was only enough to get him to the airport. He decided to fill it completely, which he did, so he'd have enough for the return journey. With the above completed, he felt that all the necessary preparations were in place.

The first disappointment occurred when he hit the M62. There was a thin blanket of fog. Cars and lorries were tail to bonnet and the overhead directions were to slow down to forty mph. In fact, they were just crawling. As they passed every junction, he hoped that the road beyond would be clear, but that was not to be. The stretch to Manchester, which one would expect to do in forty minutes, now lasted ninety. By this point, he was beginning to fear that he would miss his flight. But far worse, which he had not counted on during his preparation, was the working of his water pills. He drove to the next service station, rushed to the toilets, relieved himself, and then rushed back to the car to join the crawl. And it went on and on.

At 9:30, when the road ahead became clear, he was still thirty miles from the airport. He felt certain he was going to miss the flight unless it was delayed. He pressed hard on the accelerator urged on not just by trying to catch the flight, but also the far greater urge brought on by the water pills.

He got to the airport and drove into the car park, but in his confusion took the wrong lane. He had to reverse and go back around the roundabout to get into the right one.

After parking the car and rushing like a man possessed to the airport terminal, he was greeted by the announcement of his name on the tannoy and that he should make his way to Departures. But even that had to wait for his relieving the pressure in his bladder. He asked the first person he met, a cleaner, to direct him to the nearest toilets.

He came out and rushed to Departures with a final announcement telling him to go to gate number five. There was no queue at security. He told them, out of breath, that he was in a hurry, that he might be missing the flight. He must have appeared a proper sight: flustered, tired, flushed, worried and agitated. They saw him for what they look for to earn their living!

They swept him with the metal detector several times. They got him to remove his shoes, which they examined carefully. They had him lift his feet in turn to be looked at and prodded, while jacket, fleece and scarf were examined thoroughly by more than one person. As soon as they finished, he picked up his things and rushed to gate five where he was directed to the last bus that was waiting for him.

Fortunately, the flight was delayed. A steward rearranged the luggage in one of the overhead lockers and helped him stow his case and jacket. He took the last unoccupied aisle seat and waited for take-off, the permission to undo the seat belt and the opportunity to beat everyone else to the toilet. As he settled into the seat utterly exhausted, he remembered that his mobile had been ringing while he was driving, which he had ignored, and that he no longer had his scarf. He'd had time to check and recheck the list several times, ticking off the stages that had been negotiated already and marking what remained outstanding, After landing he retrieved his case and jacket from the locker, but there was no doubt that the scarf was lost.

He was visibly confused when he reached passport control. The immigration officer was a stern, middle-aged woman. As he extended the open passport, he asked if he was at "terminal un ou deux". The official sternness dissolved into an indulgent wide-open smile as she replied, "Two!"

He made his way to the Europcar offices. He thought of telephoning his son for the reference but didn't think he could manage it. He was in a hurry to get to the desk, trailing his case. He would have to find a seat, sit down, get out his pocket diary to look up his son's mobile number and at the same time find some paper in his pocket on which to jot it down while doubting if he could find a pen.

There wasn't what one would call a queue at Europcar. There were three desks each manned by a woman clerk attending to a customer or pair of customers. There was no obvious queuing system. He stood facing the middle desk at a decent distance and started to fiddle with his mobile trying to dial 901 hoping to hear his son's message, which he would then answer by simply pressing one key. A big, determined brute of a man came in and stood close to him. It was obvious that, come what may, the brute was going to beat him to the next table that became free. He judged him by his looks and the way he carried himself as one who, thinking himself superior, would see nothing wrong in cheating the widow, stealing from the blind, kicking the crutch off the lame, crushing the old – and thinking they deserved it!

As soon as a desk became available, the man rushed to it faster than him pressing the 9 of 901. Of the other two desks, he guessed the end one held better promise. The clerk manning it struck him as being more business-like. Soon, he was sitting across from her. She was black (sort of) colonial, more colonial than black, probably in her mid- or upper-forties. She spoke slowly with a cultured, reassuring voice and what he perceived to be a slightly unorthodox accent emerging at the ending of words. He was struck by her and her serenity.

He bent down and nervously unzipped his case, took out the bundle of papers and money, removed the rubber bands holding them together, and then produced his driving licence. He added the passport from his inner jacket pocket, which he gathered in one hand while the other held his mobile and credit card.

While he was doing this, the woman looked at him calmly and asked quizzically, "*Vous êtes seul?*" to which he nodded. She took his passport, had it photographed and then looked at the driving licence before returning the two. After starting to trawl the computer, she stopped and said there was a little problem with the system. She got up, moved away and started to talk softly into her mobile. When she stopped, he flourished his own mobile. He told her that it was his son who had made the booking, so he would now call him to get the reference. She said she didn't need the reference, it was there in her computer, just that there was a small technical problem to resolve. She asked him if he would sit on a bench close by so she could attend to other clients while he waited. She said those words with the same calm and reassuring serenity as before. He got up and commented how heavy the air was; she agreed that it was uncomfortable.

He went across to the bench, took off his jacket and sat down resignedly. He was confused, as if in a dream, but felt no anger, no disappointment. At the same time he realised (he knew the feeling) that he was not fully in control. He kept checking and rechecking that his credit card was in its usual place in his wallet, that the passport was now in his shirt breast pocket, that he still had in the same pocket the 2,90 euros for the toll, and that his driving licence and banknotes were in the case tied together by the rubber bands as before.

Then he remembered. He realised that the problem was the argument he'd had over a damage insurance claim on an earlier Europcar hire. He rose and walked across to tell the clerk what the problem was, that it had been resolved culminating in his paying the sum in question. He commented on the perennial problems associated with the damage excess and insurance, and she agreed that it was a nuisance. He repeated that the problem had been resolved. For confirmation, he got out his French chequebook to show her the stub of the cheque that he had sent to Europcar, but he wasn't sure which one it was. She told him not to worry, that an enquiry had been sent to their accounts department and she would let him have the car as soon as they came back with a clearance.

He returned to the bench and relaxed. There was a lull. There were no more customers. The colonial walked over to the other table for a chat. She seemed popular even as she looked superior. He was struck by the way she walked – not walked, but glided. He was sitting there for a long time, perhaps an hour or more. She came across and brought him a bottle of mineral water. For the first time that day, even as he waited, he felt happy. Happy to be sitting there, time suspended, looking at her, ignoring everything else. There was her slim body, which she carried with dignity, the way her wild colonial hair was held together, the discreet earrings, the silver or steel bangles, the couple of rings on her fingers, the colour of her skin – and her big brown eyes.

Eventually the clearance came; she motioned to him and he walked across. She suggested that he sat down, which he did. He bent down, opened his case and got out the bundle containing the driving licence with passport. She said she had already noted them. After he returned the bundle to his case, she pointed to the rubber bands on the table that he had forgotten to reuse. She then got down to the business. She asked him if he wanted to add damage waiver insurance, and he nodded. She mentioned a figure, and he said it was all right. She asked if he wanted to pay for a full tank, and he nodded. She said how much everything came to, and he nodded. He was barely taking in what she was saying. He was enchanted by her voice, her calm, her serenity. He heard himself say, "*Que vous êtes gentille!*" He then added, as if to himself, "*Si belle!*" What he was then seeing was not a clerk at a car hire firm, but a picture of beauty along with a calm, serene, unhurried, warm world.

In reality, the words were not addressed to her, nor did she appear to react to them, except that there was a slight change to the colour of her eyes and to the light reflected from them. She asked him to sign the contract and then handed him the car key saying it was in bay F11 on the first floor. She asked if he would be coming back. He did not understand. She corrected herself and asked if he knew how to get back. He nodded. He reminded her that she had returned the credit card without taking payment. Her calm deserted her for a brief moment before she took back the card and processed the payment. He thanked her, got up and made his way to take the lift to the first floor.

As he waited for the lift, he turned around and saw her glide towards him. He said jokingly, "Have you come to show me the way?" She disavowed that by gesture rather than words. He took it that she did not want to embarrass him by stating the obvious, that he was a frail, confused old man who needed help. The impression she gave implied that she was undertaking independent business, except that they were going the same way.

Turning right towards D, E and F, she walked ahead while he followed with his case on wheels a couple of metres behind, his eyes fixed on her good figure and poise. After D she turned to E, and he followed. They turned to F where he saw the odd numbers to his left. He started to count them silently to himself: *thirty-one, twenty-nine, twenty-seven*. When he reached eleven, she was standing by the car. He asked if it was his car, and she nodded. After she opened the boot, he put in his case and jacket. While he was doing that, she busied herself examining all around the car. She exclaimed when she saw a scratch. He did not react and took no notice. She asked him for his copy of the contract and noted the scratch along with her initials. He opened the driver's door and stepped in with trepidation wondering if he would recognise and be able to handle the controls. She opened the passenger door and looked in to see if he needed any help. He turned on what he thought was the light switch but nothing happened. She suggested that he put the key in the ignition first. Once he did, he was relieved to see the lights come on and to find the right switch that operated the window on his side, which he would need to lower at the toll barrier. She told him to wait for her to close the boot before starting the engine. When she came back, he leaned across extending his arm and they shook hands over the well of the car. She then closed the passenger door and glided away. He spent a couple of minutes familiarising himself with the car and checking the mirrors. He got out the toll money, which he counted. He then drove forward and turned right. Some twenty metres ahead, she was waiting and pointing towards the way out. He waved to her and she waved back. When he last looked in the rear mirror, before turning away, she was still standing following the car with her eyes.

The drive along the autoroute was uneventful. At Maréchal Juin, he stopped at the supermarket to buy groceries. He parked the car in the only vacant bay next to the entrance. But when he came out, he could not find the car. He walked along the line of parked cars, car key in hand, looking for it.

A middle-aged woman, seeing him approach her car while pointing a car key in its direction, called out asking if he had lost his car. She said this mischievously with a laugh. After he apologised, she laughed again. He turned back as he realised that the door by which he had come out was not the one he had gone through originally.

He felt on home territory as he turned the key in the door of the apartment. After an urgent visit to the bathroom, water pills working overtime, he opened the shutters and French windows, carried the tables and chairs to the terrace, turned on the water heater, made himself a cup of tea, and then telephoned the children.

Later, he drove to Papa Nino for a light meal, and then came back to sit on the terrace with a drink. Looking up to the sky, a plane was gliding down towards Nice airport. It looked so tiny and insignificant – yet he thought of the hundreds of worlds within it.

Then he remembered the warfarin.

❄ ❄ ❄

The First Night

He drew back the bolt and opened the front door, saw the man first, then saw her as she darted through and rushed up the stairs, quick as lightning. But he saw enough to take in the thin, rumpled nightdress, the torn hem, the bare feet, the bare legs with thin streaks of red. The man said he saw her by the cricket club. He understood: Park Avenue, across Soldiers Field, then the narrow footpath overgrown with bramble. He thanked the man, and then the latter, visibly embarrassed, walked away.

She was in bed when he reached upstairs, only her face showing from under the covers, her eyes closed. He sat on the edge of the bed and asked if she was all right. She opened her eyes and said she was asleep. He asked if she would like a cup of tea.

She said, "What about the children?"

He answered that they were fine, all happily at home with their parents.

She said, "But where are the children?"

"They're fine, nothing to worry about," he said.

"Water," she said.

He went downstairs to get some. On the way he rang Phyllis. He went back upstairs and propped her up to take in the water.

Hearing knocks at the front door, she became agitated, pushed away the tumbler, sank back and crept under the covers. He pulled them back and told her not to worry. He went down and told the two women at the door that she was with him; he would give them a call in the morning. They gave him pills in a paper pouch. He went up again and told her that Phyllis was on her way.

She said, "I know who you are!"

"Who am I?"

"You are Dad."

"That's right."

"What about the children?"

"Everything is fine. You don't need to worry."

"You're Dad."

"That's right. Phyllis will be here soon."

"Are you sure they're all right?"

"Yes, quite sure – nothing to worry about."

She took in a deep breath, closed her eyes and rolled aside, and then sat up with a start at the sound of the back door opening.

"Who is that?"

"That will be Phyllis."

She came running up the stairs and pulled back the bed-covers. "What's this, then? What have you done to yourself? Look at all those scratches."

She went to the bathroom and came back with a wet towel. He went downstairs and came up with tea on a tray. He handed her the paper pouch.

He was sitting in the kitchen when Phyllis came down ready to leave.

"I've given her a wash, changed her and changed the sheets," she said.

"Have you given her the pills? Did she swallow them?"

"Yes, with the usual struggle."

She made him a mug of tea and brought it to the table. "I have to go. She's settled now. You can understand, it being the first night. You want to get yourself some sleep. It's well past midnight. I'll be back at eight, before they come."

He went up again and went to sit at her bedside. Her eyes were half-closed. "Are you sleepy?" he asked.

“Where are they?”

“You just stop worrying. Everything is fine.”

“They say he has jaundice.”

“But that was such a long time ago, John is fine. He is grown now with a family of his own.”

“We had a holiday.”

“You remember our first holiday in Filey?”

“The seaside.”

“That’s right. Do you remember Rebecca playing the machines at Pat Corrigan?”

“The machines.”

“And John digging in the sand, day after day – thinking to get all the way to Australia?”

“The sandpit.”

“How clever of you, the sandpit at the Coach House.”

“I know who you are.”

“Who am I?”

“Fwad.”

“That’s right, you always said it that way.”

“Do not leave me.”

“I shall never leave you.”

“What about the children?”

“Don’t worry. Everything is as it should be.”

“I know who you are.”

“Who am I, then?”

“You are Dad.”

“Did you like Filey?”

“Where are they?”

“Everything is fine. There’s nothing to worry about.”

“Are you sure?”

“Quite sure. I asked you about Filey. Would you like us to go back to Filey?”

“Do we have the money?”

"We have lots of money."

She smiled. "Lots of money!"

"Do you remember the time when we were young?"

"They are very young. Will they survive?"

"What a strange thought. They are grown with children of their own."

"Where are they?"

"You came every day to have lunch with me in Covent Garden. Do you remember?"

"The Market."

"You worked at the BBC. Do you remember?"

"The BBC."

"The Langham. Audience research."

"Miss Williams."

"That's right. She was your manager."

"The Langham."

"That's right. That's where you worked. Do you remember?"

"Miss Williams."

"I was in potatoes."

"We had lunch."

"We discovered the apple strudel, do you remember?"

"Apple strudel."

"You liked the apple strudel."

"Clove."

"You came every day at lunch time."

"Lunchtime."

"That's right, you came to lunch."

"Lunch."

"The Masons Arms."

"Pub."

"You remember where I worked? An office upstairs?"

"Stairs."

"You remember Luis Matutano?"

"Spanish."

"That's right. That's who I worked for."

"Spanish people."

"You remember the secretary?"

"What?"

"Her name was Lolita, came from Gibraltar."

"Loleechi."

"That's right, you are brilliant. That's what she called herself."

"She is fat."

"Do you remember us one day, after lunch, stopping outside a jewellers? It was payday, cost me two pounds."

"Forty-five shillings!" she said with a wicked smile.

"You looked in the window and pointed to a ring."

"A gold ring."

"I said, 'Do you like it?' and you nodded."

"A gold ring."

"That's right, a plain gold ring."

"A wedding ring."

He took her left hand in his. "This is it, here now, the plain gold ring, on your finger, as it has been for fifty years."

"I know who you are."

"Who am I, then?"

"You are Fwad."

"That's how you always said it."

She was suddenly distraught, and emitted a cry.

"What's the matter?"

She emitted another cry.

"Can I do anything for you?"

Another cry, eyes wide open with a look of dread.

"You're having bad thoughts, a nightmare."

"Stay with me."

"I shall never leave you. Everything is fine. Nothing to worry about." He lifted the end of the covers and slipped into bed. "It is just a bad dream. Everything is fine. Now just relax and go to sleep."

"You will not leave me?"

He turned towards her, took her left hand and held it. "You see, we shall always be together."

"I know who you are."

"Who am I, then?"

"You are Dad."

"Now forget the bad dream, close your eyes and go to sleep."

He could tell by the rhythm of her breathing that she was fast asleep.

He slipped out of the bed and put on a dressing gown over the top of his shirt and trousers. He went to sit in the easy chair at the table by the window, then got back up to pick a book from the shelf, came back and switched on the table lamp. He opened the book of verse, which made no sense, then got up, walked across silently to see that she was still asleep before returning to the easy chair. He turned off the light and closed his eyes.

He awoke to the sound of knocking. Dawn ablaze in the oak tree. Poetry prostrate at his feet.

* * *